THE GREAT GOLD COMEBACK

By James R. Cook

**Updated
and
Expanded
March 1998**

165,000 Copies in Circulation

Published by Newsletter Systems,
  5000 Green Lane,
  P.O. Box 11206,
  St. Paul, MN 55111.

Design and typesetting by Blue Book Publications.
Production supervision by Paul G. Wichtendahl
Project management by Gordie Rasmussen

ISBN: 0-9641917-2-5

TABLE OF CONTENTS

ACKNOWLEDGEMENTS

The first three chapters of this book are a rewrite of Donald Hoppe's 1972 book, "How To Invest In Gold Stocks And Avoid The Pitfalls". When I began putting this volume together, I called Mr. Hoppe and asked if I could quote extensively from the first several chapters of his book. He suggested I rewrite it in my own words. Consequently I have condensed, rewritten and added additional facts.

INTRODUCTION

Gold holds less appeal to the U.S. public these days than at anytime in the past twenty-five years and perhaps less than ever before in U.S. history. At such a nadir of its influence the need for gold is greater than ever. That would make sense from a contrary opinion standpoint. In a nation where self-indulgence, bizarre behavior, over-consumption, gambling, stimulants, narcotics, mindless entertainment, marginal integrity, and crime are commonplace, gold would be of small interest.

In an age of victims, welfarism, redistribution, government paternalism, political correctness, something for nothing, left-wing economics, and a de-emphasis of merit, gold would attract few advocates.

In a country with record low savings and investment, runaway public and private debt, gargantuan budget and trade deficits and grossly over-speculated securities markets, gold would have few followers.

The wealthiest nation in the world has become the most dysfunctional. A great leveling lies ahead. Don't confuse these views with the oddballs who carry billboards that proclaim "The end is near." There will always be an America and a dollar - even if a dollar only buys you a piece of bubble gum. What I am saying is that the end of America as we know it is near. Things will be different after a stock market crash: painfully high interest rates, a bond market disaster, plunging asset values, severe price inflation, a debt meltdown, government defaults, a collapsing dollar, a depression, and widespread panic and crisis.

Frankly, we deserve this ferocious comeuppance. Everywhere you look in America there is dependency, financial excess, profligacy, intemperance, grossness, indolence, bad manners, arrogance and incivility. In the long run the nation will be better off after suffering the effects of the great financial meltdown that lies ahead.

Unfortunately, many will be hurt, and the ability to survive financially will depend on foresight and mental toughness. This book is written for the nimble few who will be the financial survivors in the stressful future. They will benefit the most from the great gold comeback.

CHAPTER I

GOLD AND CIVILIZATION

"The desire for gold is the most universal and deeply rooted commercial instinct of the human race."

Gerald M. Loeb

"Gold was not selected arbitrarily by governments to be the monetary standard. Gold had developed for many centuries on the free market as the best money; as the commodity providing the most stable and desirable monetary medium."

Murray N. Rothbard

"Even during the period when Rome lost much of her ancient prestige, an Indian traveler observed that trade all over the world was operated with the aid of Roman gold coins which were accepted and admired everywhere."

Paul Einzig

Gold retains importance today but no longer influences history the way it once did. In this century, governments have reduced the monetary role of gold. Lenin scorned gold and promised to make bathroom fixtures with gold. Keynesian economists who influence U.S. economic policy consider it an unworkable relic. Gold ownership by U.S. citizens has fallen since the early 1980's. This will change soon, and in the late 1990's gold will be restored to greater prominence than at any other time in recent U.S. history. The failure of the dollar will set in motion a spectacular comeback for gold and launch a renewed age of influence for the yellow metal.

Gold has always occupied an important place in human affairs. Nations flourished with gold as money and entire cultures died off without it. The wealth and power of ancient Persia can be linked to the Persian gold coin, the Daric. Their gold money brought them commercial success. When Alexander the Great conquered the Persians, he used the gold he captured to further his military objectives.

Early civilizations that relied on gold achieved great success. The Byzantine Empire lasted for 800 years based on its gold coin, the Bezant. It was no coincidence that shortly after eliminating gold coinage, The Byzantine Empire disappeared. The economy of ancient Rome became a shambles once they debased the purity and value of their coinage. The great Spanish empire rose and fell with the amount of gold they extracted from the Americas.

The history of gold serves as a road map to the progress of civilization. Gold money fuels commerce and sparks those rare but important bursts of progress that highlight the ages. Valuable historical artifacts made of gold testify to gold's role as the supreme metal of the arts. It continues to this day to be an industrial commodity and high fashion adornment of great value.

Since gold is easily worked, jewelers and artisans prize the lustrous yellow metal. Gold remains unaffected by water or oxygen. It neither rusts nor corrodes. Unlike silver, gold does not tarnish. It is virtually imperishable and one of the most stable elements. Its density and softness afford it a wealth of uses. An ounce of gold can be stretched into a wire 50 miles long. It can be pounded into a flat sheet as big as a house. It can plate a copper wire for 1,000 miles. Gold conducts electricity so well that a microscopic amount can replace miles of wiring inside a computer. If it were cheaper in price its uses would multiply beyond measure.

Even before gold was used as money, it was considered as the ultimate form of wealth for kings, merchants, and the early church. Gold was the first substance mentioned in the Bible. Gold artifacts and jewelry have been found that date back 6,000 years. Fabulous gold treasures were found in the tomb of King Tut. The Pharaoh's body was encased in a coffin made from 25,000 ounces of solid gold.

Nothing else in history served to display wealth, power, and prestige as did gold jewelry and gold artifacts that were the epitome of early art and craftsmanship.

The great archaeologist Heinrich Schlieman made enough money in the California gold rush to help finance his excavation of Troy and Mycenae. After discovering a golden death mask he wired authorities "I have looked upon the face of Agamemnon." The golden treasures he dug up at Troy were housed in a Berlin museum and removed in 1945 by the Russians. They were thought to have been melted into bars. The new Russian government recently hinted that these priceless artifacts may still be stored in Moscow.

Among early civilizations, gold evolved into a prized possession. Beauty and scarcity enhanced mankind's desire for it. A tiny amount of gold took on a high value. Great wealth could now be safely stored in a small hiding place. It could be buried and not rot. It was impervious to moisture and dampness. These factors were instrumental in the transforming of gold from an item of value into the role of money.

Prior to the evolution of money, barter was the primary means of negotiating a transaction. An exchange of cattle for grain or weapons could prove cumbersome. A medium of exchange that stored value and acted as a unit of account could make commercial life far easier.

Money has been everything from sea shells to beads. In modern times cigarettes and chocolate have temporarily served as money. Gold stood out. No one turned down gold. No one could get enough of it. Nothing else provided the deep seated psychological satisfaction of gold. Furthermore, the yellow metal could be broken into small units, each having a high value. It was durable and portable. More than any other form of money, gold built confidence. It established a solid underpinning for trade and commerce. When gold first began to serve as money, it must surely have been responsible for a great boom in commercial activity, and was thus a principle engine of human progress.

About 2,000 years before Christ, the early Babylonians developed a system of weights and measures that added greatly to the ability of gold to serve as money. The Babylonian shekel, a small gold bar, became the common monetary unit. The shekel enabled the Babylonians to dominate commercial activity in the fertile crescent (modern Iraq) and build an important early culture. While it was the Babylonians who created gold bars, it was a small, short-lived kingdom (in what is now Turkey) that invented coinage. This was Lydia, the country of the legendary monarch, Croesus. In approximately 55 BC, Lydia struck the first gold coins. These crude lumps of pure gold were quickly imitated by the Greeks, who were soon to strike the first silver coins. The use of coins expanded rapidly from the Mediterranean to the Mideast. The Greeks elevated the engraving and minting of coins to a high art form.

The Romans never seemed to get the hang of stable money. They were the first major inflators in history. Rome constantly experimented with clipping or debasing its coinage. The Romans tried to engineer a form of money that could be debased without a corresponding loss of value. They watered down the purity of their coinage but strived to keep the purchasing power intact. Sounds familiar doesn't it?

One exception was Julius Caesar, who upon taking control of the Roman Republic, introduced a gold standard. His coinage, the Aureus, brought on a period of financial calm that lasted almost a century. Subsequent emperors, however, diluted the coinage once again. It did not occur to the Romans that a sound and honorable monetary unit could keep their empire together through means other than force. Inflation, as much as any other factor, contributed to the downfall of the Roman Empire. Historians often draw comparisons between Rome and modern day currency debasement.

CHAPTER II

GOLD AND WESTERN EUROPE

"The history of fiat money is little more than a register of monetary follies and inflations. Our present age merely affords another entry in this dismal register."

Hans F. Sennholz

"As fewer and fewer people have confidence in paper as a store of value, the price of gold will continue to rise."

Jerome F. Smith

"Those entrapped by the herd instinct are drowned in the deluges of history. But there are always the few who observe, reason, and take precautions, and thus escape the flood. For these few gold has been the asset of last resort."

Antony C. Sutton

Prosperity and progress flourish with widespread monetary use of gold. The stability of gold money brings about dramatic commercial and cultural advancements. Social and political upheavals have been rare under a gold standard. Sustained economic progress seems to require gold coinage or gold backed money.

The emergence of the Italian City States in the 13th Century led to a period of enlightenment and a rich cultural renaissance. Human progress had come to a standstill during six centuries of the dark ages. At first, Florence, and then Venice, issued gold coins. There followed a period of prosperity that pulled Western Europe out of the doldrums.

Unfortunately in the centuries that followed, the monarchs and rulers of England and the Continent developed a fondness for clipping and debasing their coins. This pilferage worked much better than the alchemists who promised to transmute base metals into gold. Centuries of chronic debasement from dishonest rulers contributed to the economic stagnation of feudalism.

The influx of gold into Spain from the new world was at the heart of a burst of economic activity that swept through Europe in the 16th century. Spain flourished, its timeless art and literature personified by Velasquez and Cervantes. Once the gold stopped flowing out of Mexico and South America, Spain declined as rapidly as it had vaulted to prominence.

No matter how much gold had been funneled into Spain, there was always a cry for more. Throughout history complaints about the scarcity of money have been commonplace. Cures for this shortage are invariably schemes to dilute the existing money stock, despite the fact that creating more money cannot by itself increase the wealth of the people. Gold meets the most stringent definitions of liquid wealth, and this pure form of money can only be produced through an elaborate mining process. In fact, a slow increase in gold money through mining seems vastly preferable to the printing press method of money creation, since the former has a natural brake on expansion, while the latter has no such safeguard.

The view that more and more money must be made available in order to expand the economy is a myth. It's in a recession or depression that the cry for new money becomes loudest. But the unbridled expansion of money creates an unhealthy boom in the first place. The liquidation of the excesses of the boom leads to a bust. If the money supply remains stable, as with gold, then increased production will cause prices for goods to drop. That's just one of the many benefits of sound money, in contrast to the inflationary tricks of modern government.

Paper money made its appearance slightly over 300 years ago. This early money was a receipt from a goldsmith who kept a safe storage place for gold. These receipts came to be circulated widely as a method of payment. The U.S. government used similar gold certificates in the 19th and early 20th centuries, redeemable in gold owned by the government.

At the beginning of the 17th century, banks began to experiment with the issuance of bank credit as a means of payment. Governments rapidly latched on to this practice of creating fiat money as a way to pay off their debt. In eighteenth century France this resulted in two of the worst hyper-inflations in history. These hyper-inflations led to the French Revolution, a period of political, social and financial chaos which enabled Napoleon Bonaparte to take power. Sometimes, periods of monetary upheaval bring on dictatorship.

Major gold discoveries by the 49'ers in California soon made enough of the yellow metal available to put the world on a gold standard. With money creation out of the hands of the politicians, the industrial revolution gave birth to our modern era. Enough gold was mined in Alaska, the Yukon, and in South Africa by the end of the 19th century, to make gold coinage widespread throughout the world. This period of great economic growth dramatically increased living standards for millions of Americans, attracting a steady influx of immigrants to share in the wealth and opportunity of capitalism. In terms of productivity, enhanced living conditions (starvation eliminated and pestilence controlled), no period in history can compare with that time in which America lived under the gold standard. Economic growth catapulted forward with dynamic increases year after year.

Unfortunately, governments the world over invariably abolished the discipline of gold when emergencies arose. It is a measure of the corruption of modern governments how often they resort to currency debasement.

Loose money and credit policies financed the futility and waste of the first world war and led to a breakdown of the gold standard. The Germans, who were left destitute by the war, experimented with fiat money and introduced one of the great hyper-inflations in history. Large quantities of paper currency were issued in Germany throughout the early 1920's, eventually driving daily price levels to astronomical levels. A German supposedly wheeled a baby-buggy full of money to her local bakery to buy a loaf of bread. She left it outside for a moment while she went in to the bakery. When she came out, someone had dumped the money onto the street and had stolen the buggy.

The destructive German inflation sowed the seeds of national discord that proved fertile ground for the National Socialists and Hitler. So often in history, a period of monetary chaos enables an extremist to take power. After the second world war in China the Nationalists fought to stay in control while inflation raged. They paid their army with paper money. Mao-Tse-Tung paid his army with silver coin. Ultimately, his Red army evicted the Nationalists from China and they fled to Formosa (Taiwan). Those citizens who had paper money couldn't get out of the country. Those who had gold were able to buy passage out when the Red army rolled across China.

CHAPTER III

GOLD IN AMERICA

"For more than two thousand years gold's natural qualities made it man's universal medium of exchange. In contrast to political money, gold is honest money that survived the ages and will live on long after the political fiats of today have gone the way of all paper."

Hans F. Sennholz

"When paper money systems begin to crack at the seams, the run to gold could be explosive."

Harry Browne

"A sustained policy of inflation leads a gold-standard country to a cumulative loss of gold and finally to the abandonment of that system; then the national currency can freely depreciate. In a country whose currency is not convertible into gold, inflation leads to its continuous devaluation in terms of foreign currencies."

Michael A. Heilperin

In colonial America, gold coins were scarce. Early colonists relied on beaver pelts, tobacco, musket balls, gun powder, and rum for money and barter. The principal silver coin was the Spanish silver dollar. The colonists cut the Spanish dollar into halves and quarters to make smaller denominations. From this practice came the term "Two bits" and "Four bits".

The Revolutionary War forced our poor nation to issue the continental dollar, a paper currency unbacked by gold. After the war these continental dollars soon became worthless. The new constitution mandated production of silver dollars and gold coins in denominations of 2 1/2 dollars, 5 dollars and 10 dollars. The first U.S. mint located in Philadelphia began stamping out this gold coinage in 1792. Early gold discoveries in California provided an ample supply of gold in America and fostered a de facto gold standard. Although the gold standard became an official government act in 1900, the United States had been on a gold standard since 1830.

Economist Hans Sennholz states. "The gold standard is as old as civilization. Throughout the ages, the gold standard emerged again and again because man needed a dependable medium of exchange. Gold provided such a medium. It was the most marketable good that gradually gained universal employment - and thus became money. It's natural qualities, i.e., its use for the manufacture of ornaments and jewelry, its easy divisibility, great durability, storability and transportability, made this precious metal well suited to serve as money.

The U.S. divorced itself from the gold standard during The Great Depression. Credit expansion throughout the 1920's made it impossible to redeem these newly created dollars for gold. The gold reserves were not large enough. The stock market crash, bank failures, and bankruptcies, created a demand for gold. Panic and fear caused depositors to withdraw gold and currency to the point that there were runs on many banks. Rather than massively devalue the dollar to maintain gold convertibility, the newly elected Roosevelt administration declared a bank holiday.

This emergency order was followed a few days later by an executive order to all citizens demanding the surrender of all gold coins, gold bullion, and gold certificates, to the Federal Reserve within 25 days. Failure to comply was punishable by 10 years in prison and a large fine. The game plan was to stabilize the dollar in world exchange markets. The seizure of gold gave the government large enough reserves to retain international convertibility. Foreign governments could convert dollars into the gold, but U.S. citizens could not. Roosevelt hoped that this would make the dollar sound. Ultimately, (40 years later) even foreign governments were denied this convertibility.

After World War II, the economic philosophy of John Maynard Keynes prevailed in Western Europe, and the U.S. Keynes had no use for gold and recommended that it be divorced from money. This philosophy helped lead to widespread inflation. Subsequently, over the past 50 years, the dollar has lost more than 90% of its purchasing power.

When the international gold standard was abolished, it was replaced by a paper standard. Variations of the paper standard exist today and have allowed the U.S. to run large trade deficits. Consumption of overseas goods far exceeds our exports. Consequently, we have become a debtor nation.

In his 1987 book, "Beyond Our Means", Wall Street Journal Editor, Alfred A. Malabre, Jr. writes, "Our willingness, even determination to live beyond our means - to go far more deeply into debt than our resources safely will allow - has led to ominous patterns."

Writing in 1970, Author Gordon L. Weil put it this way. "A country cannot always spend more abroad than it receives from foreign countries. If it did so, it would soon go broke. A government might try, of course, to print more currency in hopes of using it to finance additional foreign purchases, but as soon as other nations found out that they were being paid with worthless 'printing-press money,' they would refuse to accept any more."

Alfred Malabre, Jr. continues, " if America sinks deeper and deeper into debtor-nation status, painful bills will begin coming due. Americans will be compelled to give up more and more of their income simply to pay interest to overseas creditors."

Gordon Weil sums it up. "Confidence is a fragile flower; it withers whenever there is the slightest change of temperature in the monetary atmosphere. A country must in the long run break even in its transactions with other countries or people will begin to doubt its ability to maintain the value of its money and its economic place in the world. Its government has to make sure, through the national economic policy, and in fact, through every other policy, ranging from trade through defense, that it is not a chronic debtor. Many governments believe it is also their job to say things are going just fine, even when they are not. This approach only makes the fall from grace harder when it comes, as it inevitably does."

The U.S. has managed year after year to run-up unmanageable trade deficits with only minimal damage to the dollar in foreign exchange markets. How long foreigners will, or can continue to swallow $160 billion of our money or more each year is an open question. This process can not be sustained for much longer. The threat to the value of the dollar can't be overstated. When a dollar plunge begins in earnest, gold will tend to directly offset this loss.

Alfred Malabre, Jr. concludes, "In brief, the jig is about up and, for all the accumulated wisdom of all the eminent economists of the various schools, painless extrication from our predicament just isn't going to be possible. To be sure, the economic bind that now grips us will be broken in time but only through an intense amount of economic dislocation and downright pain. Just what degree of pain is unclear, but it will arrive, one way or another.

"However, the bind is broken - through inflation or deflation or otherwise - living standards will suffer, in some households more than in others. Unemployment will mount. Most importantly, financial obligations will be disregarded on a massive scale, for there will be no orderly way to liquidate debts."

The lack of interest in gold on the part of the American public at such a critical juncture in the history of our currency should appeal to all contrary-opinion investors. At perhaps the most crucial time in U.S. history, for a citizen to own gold, the yellow metal bores the financial experts and mystifies the public.

Furthermore, gold is seldom, if ever, given much thought in government circles. The U.S. gold reserves are rarely mentioned in Washington affairs. Politicians have little or no understanding of the role of gold. In the 1980's a United States Senator suggested that our gold reserves be sold off to depress gold prices and punish South Africa. He gave up the idea because low gold prices would also harm U.S. gold mining companies. He was ignorant of the fact that U.S. gold reserves are part of the national patrimony and still act as a de facto reserve behind the dollar.

In a monetary crisis, foreigners and investors who hold dollars may want to know exactly how many ounces of gold stand behind the U.S. dollar. If our government ever sells off the U.S. gold reserve it could mean that the dollar would plunge further and lose its role as the world's reserve currency. Once the dollar loses its value through devaluation or hyper-inflation, any new currency would need this gold for convertibility, or it would fare no better than the ruined currency it replaces.

CHAPTER IV

GOLD TO THE PRESENT

"Until government administrators can so identify the interests of government with those of the people and refrain from defrauding the masses through the device of currency depreciation for the sake of remaining in office, the wiser ones will prefer to keep as much of their wealth in the most stable and marketable forms possible - forms which only the precious metals provide."

Elgin Groseclose

"Gold would have value if for no other reason than that it enables a citizen to fashion his financial escape from the state."

William F. Rickenbacker

"America today has insufficient savings to finance both crucial investment and its consumption of imports."

James Dale Davidson

Since gold cannot be created from thin air, its use as money tends to keep government spending in check. By removing this gold discipline from the U.S. currency, politicians could more easily create money to pay for new spending. When government needs only to make a bookkeeping entry to get new money to pay bills, inflation is virtually guaranteed. It's too tempting for politicians not to spend money on projects that harmonize with their political goals, or to reward their constituents.

Fiat money dovetailed nicely with the prevalent political philosophy that gained influence in the U.S. after the second world war. Building on the initiatives of the Roosevelt administration, the government aimed to take an even greater role in solving national problems and regulating the economy. Thus sprang up our social welfare policy and the promise of a guaranteed life. This something for nothing philosophy grew into a wide range of government entitlements. From the beginning, this policy led to excessive government spending, which continues to worsen to this day.

In the 1960's government spending began to run away. Although political candidates promised to balance the budget and cut programs, none ever did. As the government spent more than it brought in through taxes, it began to borrow heavily in the capital markets. Over several decades, the budget deficit grew to annual amounts that were impossible to comprehend. The national debt (the accumulation of yearly deficits) soared into the trillions of dollars.

Meanwhile, the U.S. Central Bank, the Federal Reserve, intermittently launched vast expansions in the money supply to cure periodical economic slumps and to help finance or liquidate the governments debt. This led to severe rounds of price inflation that eroded the value of the dollar.

Alarmed about the damaging monetary trends that were unfolding in the 1960's, the economist Henry Hazlitt wrote in an October, 1963, issue of Newsweek, "The basic assumption of all governments today is that they not only have the right but the duty to tamper constantly with the national money. This is known as monetary management. They reject the only real solution (to sound money) - a return to a full international gold standard. They repeat the old charge that this was the system which broke down after WWI and led to the currency chaos of the '30's. The gold standard did not break down; it was deliberately abandoned and destroyed by monetary managers who wanted to dilute and inflate their national currencies, and who rightly recognized the gold standard as the great barrier to their plans. The reason governments are now opposed to a return to the full gold standard is that it would deprive them of their present powers to manage and expand - in brief, to inflate."

GOLD PRICES 1979-1997

London PM Fix

YEAR	HIGH	LOW	AVG.
1997	364.50	283.00	331.50
1996	418.00	366.00	388.00
1995	402.00	372.00	385.00
1994	402.00	370.00	386.00
1993	414.00	325.00	361.00
1992	359.60	330.35	343.76
1991	403.00	344.24	362.19
1990	423.75	345.85	383.47
1989	415.80	355.75	381.44
1988	483.90	395.30	436.93
1987	499.75	390.00	446.45
1986	438.35	326.55	367.87
1985	340.90	284.25	317.26
1984	405.85	307.50	460.44
1983	509.25	374.25	424.18
1982	481.00	296.75	375.79
1981	599.25	391.25	459.71
1980	850.00	481.50	612.56
1979	512.00	216.85	306.68

(Source: WGC, Gold Info. Cntr. & U.S. Mint)

Inflation led to a renewed interest in gold. In 1968, the gold price broke loose from its fixed rate of $35 and rose to $44. In the early 1970's gold broke out again, rising to $65 an ounce in the spring of 1972. When gold was once again legalized on January 1, 1975, gold touched the $200 an ounce mark. (Gold legalization was not all that it was cracked up to be. Americans had been vigorously buying gold coins for years that were restrikes of early coins, while the government winked at this loophole.)

Sparked by a wave of double-digit inflation in 1979-1980, gold prices soared to record levels. In February, of 1980, in a frenzy of trading activity, gold reached $850 per ounce. This price peak capped a multi-year rise that pushed gold into the investment limelight as never before. A steep decline in silver prices broke the back of the precious metals market as the government put a nasty squeeze on the Hunt brothers, who had invested heavily in silver. Inflation abated and gold prices fell off. Gold established a trading pattern throughout the balance of the 1980's between $250 and $500.

Gold prices have reacted favorably to dollar declines and to price inflation. In the early part of the 1990's gold held up reasonably well in a recession. In 1993, gold prices started up again, reached $400 and then returned to $300 in 1998.

For the future, gold should react favorably in a stock market crash or in a deflationary panic when illiquid assets are dumped on the market. Unquestionably, gold would perform well when high inflation dilutes the dollar's purchasing power, or when foreign exchange markets dramatically weaken the value of the dollar against other currencies.

Furthermore, the last few years of the 1990's are shaping up to be a period of economic crisis. Gold will likely reach new highs in the face of a general collapse of assets, a sharply devalued dollar, and a lackluster economic performance. Any kind of crisis or price inflation will augment the rush into gold.

Inflation means expansion of money and credit. It can also mean rising prices. Inflation of money and credit has been responsible for the rise in asset values. This new money went into assets and investment and did not effect consumer prices. It also went overseas to buy consumer goods (imports). In a sense the capital we exported cooled domestic price inflation but overheated Asia and helped lead to their collapse.

Throughout this decade, an enormous increase in debt drove up the stock and bond markets. This debt explosion also contributed to the economic recovery. These alarming debt levels provoked author James Dale Davidson to write, "Debt cannot go on compounding faster than output forever. At the rate it expanded in the United States in the 1980s, interest payments would consume 100 percent of GNP by the year 2015. No such thing will happen. Long before debt reaches that extreme, it will be wiped away. Either an economic deflation will cause the financial system to implode, or a political inflation of an extreme kind will obliterate much of the value of debts denominated in dollars.

"One way or the other, we expect a great reckoning. A settling of accounts. We expect the long economic boom and credit expansion that began with World War II to come to an end. The end, when it comes, will not only reveal the insolvency of many individuals and corporations, it may also bring bankruptcy to the welfare state and widespread breakdown of authority.....Such far-reaching transitions cannot occur without touching your life and the lives of those you love. More than you may now imagine, you are vulnerable to financial, economic, and political collapse."

CHAPTER V

THE SPENDING PROBLEM

"We are now reaping the bitter harvest of the poisonous seed sowed intermittently during the past....we need only take our heads out of the sand to see clearly that interventionism not only has failed to provide the promised something-for-nothing, but has led to all sorts of undesirable consequences. Indeed, many are just beginning to realize that we are moving towards disaster even though we have been on a wrong heading for decades."

Leonard Read

"Do the American voters know that the unprecedented improvement in their standard of living that the last hundred years brought was the result of the steady rise in the per-head quota of capital invested? Do they realize that every measure leading to capital decumulation jeopardizes their prosperity?"

Ludwig von Mises

"The dollar will be wiped out."

Dr. Franz Pick

Up until recently the national debt in the U.S. was increasing around $1 trillion every two years. The U.S. clearly has had a spending problem. Despite higher tax revenues from a booming stock market, deficits will reappear quickly in a recession or with any renewed spending. The cost of government programs constantly accelerate and pose a huge future problem.

While the Congress wrangles over what subsidies and programs to cut, the administration usually presents a budget that continues the spending sins of the past. Any significant spending cuts or budget surplus will be fleeting at best. The sheer scope of government almost defies meaningful reduction. Author James Turk tells us, "The size of the Federal government defies description. The sheer magnitude of the numbers is phenomenal. Can anyone meaningfully comprehend that the Federal government spends more than one thousand billion Dollars each year?" (That's a thousand five hundred billion today. He wrote this in 1991.)

Military spending comprises a large chunk of the budget, but that expenditure appears to be stubbornly receding. While the proper role of government includes protecting us against foreign aggression, it's expensive to be the world's policeman. The need to be on the cutting edge of high priced military technology doesn't exist to the extent it once did.

The biggest areas of government spending is social welfare. This category lumps together a host of entitlements, grants, and subsidies. Despite fewer people on welfare the costs of other entitlements continue to rise. Hardcore welfare recipients still get a generous government check, free housing, medical care, food stamps, and other services. These beneficiaries have a strong financial incentive to maintain a lifestyle relying solely on benefits and handouts.

As more people adopt the welfare lifestyle, social costs rise. Strains on the criminal justice system require more police, more prisons, and more judges. Hospital and medical costs rise for welfare indigents whose unhealthy life styles boost demand for free hospitalization. Medical treatment grows for addicts and victims of violence. Although they offer dubious results, psychological counseling and chemical abuse programs are widespread and expensive.

The highly charged political debate about the current reduction of welfare benefits will continue. People go bonkers when something gets taken away from them. Should the economy slow and jobs disappear don't be shocked by riots, and mayhem. The cities could suffer while incensed welfare recipients loot and pillage. We will be surprised to see meaningful cuts in welfare stick. The resistance to welfare cuts could ultimately frighten off the politicians or foster class divisions and racial animosity.

Expect to see big population shifts to those states which have the most generous welfare benefits. In high density welfare areas the upper and middle classes will move away. Certain areas of the country with low welfare populations will become meccas of prosperity and safety. The potential exists for colonies of entrepreneurial Americans to flourish in far-flung countries much like the offshore Chinese.

Social programs are not the only runaway subsidies. Through direct payments and cheap loans, agriculture appears to have the inside track on politically motivated doles. Medicare, Medicaid, student loans, low interest loans, subsidies to industries, and grants to artists, are only part of a long list of money gulping programs. These and an assortment of bizarre and unnecessary projects, bleed the government coffers dry. Only a few of these programs will ever get the knife.

Frequently the cry arises to cut government waste and make the bureaucracy more efficient. That won't work. Government doesn't have a bottom line. Unlike private enterprise, which measures results by profit or loss, government has no such yardstick. Government officials measure results by how much money they spend. That's why they always lobby for more money. *Government has no objective means to measure results.* That accounts for the gross inefficiency of bureaucracy.

Government seldom relies on merit as does business. They tend to measure employees by credentials and educational degrees. Merit often takes a back seat to political motives and to not rocking the boat. Private enterprise must constantly struggle to become more cost effective. That's why business pays close attention to the work ethic and to the merit of employees. By some estimates, private business is five to ten times more efficient than government.

When government redistributes as much money as it does, the nation becomes a hotbed of politics. Special interest groups elbow up to the government trough. Lobbyists maneuver to cash in on the bounty in Washington. Politicians and bureaucrats who control the purse strings become media stars. Payola and corruption rise. Politics flourish.

The body politic and its army of ward heelers won't give up these juicy spoils. The beneficiaries of the social welfare system and the other recipients of government spending will fight to the bitter end to maintain these privileges. The government bureaucracy never will and never can be reformed or made efficient.

Recently tax receipts from stock profits and other gains have narrowed the budget deficit. There is talk of a surplus. This will forestall serious cuts in government programs. Meaningful cuts would take money away from one person in two. It's not going to happen. However, when a faltering economy and bear market reduce tax receipts, severe cuts may be forced onto the subsidized.

Government spending is built in and uncontrollable. This runaway spending is the root cause of the decline in the dollar and of chronic inflation that lurks in the wings. Ultimately, it will wreck the dollar, impair the economy, eliminate many businesses, and reduce living standards. It will make us poorer rather than wealthier. Out-of-control spending hurts the exchange value of the dollar. As the dollar loses value against foreign currencies, gold will tend to offset this damage. The outcome of runaway social welfare and runaway government spending will lead inevitably to the destruction of the dollar and a soaring price for gold.

CHAPTER VI

THE ECONOMIST

"The way I see it, gold is headed over $1000 an ounce, probably much higher. At anywhere near current prices, it's the lowest risk, highest potential investment I can think of."

Doug Casey

"In the long run, the gold price has to go up in relation to paper money. There is no other way. To what price, that depends on the scale of the inflation - and we know that inflation will continue."

Nicholas L. Deak

"Gold bears the confidence of the world's millions, who value it far above the promises of politicians, far above the unbacked paper issued by governments as money substitutes. It has been that way through all recorded history. There is no reason to believe it will lose the confidence of people in the future."

Oakley R. Bramble

Ludwig von Mises (1881-1973) (pronounced Meesez) was born in the Austro-Hungarian empire. Hard money advocates and free market economists consider him to be the greatest economic thinker in history. He believed in limited government, the gold standard, sound money, capitalism and personal freedom. If you have never heard of him, it's time you learned more. Mises attended the University of Vienna during the high tide of the "Austrian School" of economics. His accomplishments are prodigious. In 1920, he showed that socialism and planning must fail because of the lack of market pricing. Mises insightful checkmate to collectivism was widely acknowledged when communism collapsed.

Among other things, Mises was able to show that inflation was no more than taxation and redistribution of wealth; that prices will most often fall without government induced money injections; that increases in the money supply, e.g. a sudden doubling of everyone's money holding benefits society not an iota and in fact only dilutes purchasing power; that only growth in the factors of production, land, labor, plant and equipment will increase production and standards of living.

In a brilliant and important theoretical accomplishment Mises answered a problem most economists thought unanswerable. How can we explain that the price of money is influenced by demand if to have demand it must first have a price? He traced the time component in the demand for money back in time to a useful barter commodity (e.g. silver and gold).

The dramatic implications meant money could only originate on the free market out of demand. Government, despite any attempts to the contrary, could not originate money. Money is not arbitrary pieces of paper but must originate as a useful and valuable commodity.

Mises also pointed out how central banking acts as an accomplice to government money expansion. And he began to explain his great business cycle theory. Recognizing that the market economy could not generate by itself a series of booms and busts he fixed the blame on an outside factor - the habitual expansion of money and credit.

He argued that a credit-induced boom must eventually "lead to a crack-up boom." He wrote, "The boom can last only as long as the credit expansion progresses at an ever-accelerated pace. The boom comes to an end as soon as additional quantities of fiduciary media are no longer thrown upon the loan market. But it could not last forever even if inflation and credit expansion were to go on endlessly. It would then encounter the barriers which prevent the boundless expansion of circulation credit. It would lead to the crack-up boom and the breakdown of the whole monetary system."

He warned, "The credit expansion boom is built on the sands of banknotes and deposits. It must collapse." He stated that, "If the credit expansion is not stopped in time, the boom turns into the crack-up boom; the flight into real values begins, and the whole monetary system founders. Continuous inflation (credit expansion) must finally end in the crack-up boom and the complete breakdown of the currency system."

Mises further claimed that, "Expansion (of credit) squanders scarce factors of production by malinvestment and overconsumption." Malinvestment means building shopping centers rather than factories. Overconsumption means a borrowing and spending boom by consumers that depletes savings and reduces capital investment.

Mises was aware that a credit excess could spill over into stock and bond speculation. But even he would be surprised at today's unprecedented level of credit-induced speculation. He would be depressed by the astonishing levels of public and private debt, government borrowing, central bank market interventions, trade deficits, non-bank credit growth, money velocity, illiquidity, overconsumption and foreign indebtedness. The magnitude of these excesses seemingly without penalties would appear to be rewriting the laws of economics as expressed by Mises. Trade deficits fail to harm the dollar. The stock market outperforms the economy. Capital gets used up by government and consumers at the expense of investment. Yet business rolls along. Savings are depleted but interest rates stay low. The boom seems unending, the bust postponed indefinitely. Can these phenomenon persist?

Absolutely not says Mises. "Credit expansion is not a nostrum to make people happy. The boom it engenders must inevitably lead to a debacle and unhappiness." He warns that, "Accidental, institutional, and psychological circumstances generally turn the outbreak of the crisis into a panic. The description of these awful events can be left to the historians. It is not...(our task)...to depict in detail the calamities of panicky days and weeks and to dwell upon their sometimes grotesque aspects."

"The final outcome of the credit expansion is general impoverishment. Some people may have increased their wealth; they did not let their reasoning be obfuscated by the mass hysteria, and took advantage in time of the opportunities offered by the mobility of the individual investor....but the immense majority must foot the bill for the malinvestments and the overconsumption of the boom episode."

Austrian economics rests on the foundation of readily observable human actions. Beings have goals, they set out to attain them; they have individual preferences; and they act within the framework of time. Each person and his or her actions are different and unique. The very nature of human behavior defies economic codification.

Mises points out that there are not quantitative constants in human behavior. In his greatest book, "Human Action," he developed a rational economic science based on this human factor. At the same time he tweaked the nose of today's highly popular mathematical economics, statistical economics and econometrics. This posturing and economic forecasting he dismissed as little more than poppycock.

In the early thirties, Austrian school economics was on the verge of carrying the day. But in England, the publication of John Maynard Keynes, "General Theory of Employment, Interest and Money," provided the rationalizations necessary for politicians and government to spend and inflate endlessly. Until that moment virtually the entire body and history of economic thought stood against such theories. But, Keynes theories fit hand in glove with the mentality of intervention and statism. It rationalized politicians, economists and governments jumping in bed together to expand their power and influence.

Not that Mises was rebutted or that anyone overturned his conclusions - he was simply ignored. How many Americans have ever heard of Ludwig von Mises? How many businessmen know that he placed the girders and underpinnings under free enterprise that cement that system to reason? How many know that he won the moral high ground for capitalism?

Ludwig von Mises, emigrated to the U.S. in 1940. He continued to write and lectured and taught as a visiting professor at N.Y.U. But it was a far cry from his prestige on the continent. Ignored by the media, by the academic community, by business and by government he remained undaunted, a lone figure firm of principle and intellectual courage, a genuine liberal in the classical sense.

Professor von Mises is the painstaking architect of the economy of a free society. However, mainstream economists totally ignore his blueprint. He stands far above the current arguments about how the money supply and the economy should be manipulated. For he maintains our greatest error is for government to exert any influence or control over the supply of money and the economic system.

We ignore Mises teaching at our own peril and he tells us so. "It rests with men whether they will make the proper use of the rich treasure with which this knowledge provides them or whether they will leave it unused. But if they fail to take the best advantage of it and disregard its teachings and warnings, they will not only annul economics; they will stamp out society and the human race."

CHAPTER VII

THE WELFARE PROBLEM

"In the end, more than they wanted freedom, they wanted security."

Edward Gibbon

"The paper standard is self-destructive."

Hans F. Sennholz

"With the exception only of the period of the gold standard, practically all governments of history have used their exclusive power to issue money to defraud and plunder the people."

F.A. von Hayak

Up until the 1950's welfare and government doles were frowned on by the public, and to a great extent, by welfare workers and recipients. According to author Marvin Olasky, "Before the push for a Great Society began, recipients themselves often viewed welfare as a necessary wrong....A sense of shame was relied upon to make people reluctant to accept 'the dole' unless absolutely necessary....as late as the mid-1960's, only about half of those eligible for welfare payments were receiving them...."

But liberal social workers were able to secure the levers of political power, and by the end of the 1960's, attitudes changed. Young men were taught that the dole was preferable to a low-paying job. There was no penalty for refusing work. According to a prominent social worker, "Social justice required an end to scrutiny of behavior."

Author Charles Murray tells us, "Throughout the 1970's, the conventional wisdom on the left was that scarcity of jobs was the root problem, and the provision of jobs was the root solution. But several American cities have enjoyed red-hot economies with low skill, good-paying jobs easily available...this economic growth is having almost no affect on the size of the underclass. Many of the dropouts don't even want such jobs - they are 'demeaning'....even if they pay $5 or $6 an hour."

The number of AFDC recipients doubled and redoubled again. Radical organizations established the view that welfare was a right. It was widely thought that with enough money, poverty could be cured. One liberal administration official argued, "The way to eliminate poverty is to give the poor people enough money so that they won't be poor anymore." However, the more money spent the worse the problem became.

Those trapped permanently in the welfare cycle suffer serious character damage. Excused from any requirement to accomplish anything, they experience a stifling boredom, the relief from which too often erupts in self-destructive behavior. Alcoholism and drug addiction are the most prevalent and seemingly inevitable consequence of several generations on welfare.

If a perverse dictator wished to create a psychopathic criminal class, he could do no better than to emulate the U.S. welfare system. Infants raised by mothers who are addicts, prostitutes, alcoholics, or abusers, grow up *without the powerful civilizing force of maternal love.* Says Murray, "....children unnurtured, undisciplined, sometimes unfed and unwashed....on one occasion ignored, on another laughed at indulgently, and on yet another cursed and beaten." These damaged children often grow up to be narcissistic predators.

Their crimes and the suffering they cause should be laid on the doorsteps of liberals whose runaway urge for social engineering failed to factor in the basic elements of human nature. Napoleon Hill said, "Nature does not long tolerate something for nothing." We pay a terrible price for the mistakes of social planners who refuse to truthfully examine the consequences of their programs.

Common sense tells us that something has gone radically wrong with welfare. Permanent income subsidies are chronically destructive. The problem is out of control. Thirty million people now depend on welfare.

We need to understand what causes the harmful behavior of the subsidized. In 1966, Robert Ardrey wrote a controversial inquiry into the nature of man entitled, "The Territorial Imperative". He linked behavior with the ownership and defense of territory. (Birds sing to defend their territory.) This contention, and its allusion to private property, made Ardrey unpopular with the left. His wisdom never gained mainstream attention. Nevertheless, evidence of his influence appears time and again in books on many subjects.

He wrote that there are three principal needs of all higher animals, including man: the need for identity, the need for stimulation, and the need for security. Beyond these three, he could find no others.

Ardrey wrote, "Identity, stimulation, security; if you will think of them in terms of their opposites their images will be sharpened. Identity is the opposite of anonymity. Stimulation is the opposite of boredom. Security is the opposite of anxiety. We shun anonymity, dread boredom, seek to dispel anxiety. We grasp at identification, yearn for stimulation, conserve or gain security."

"There are few exceptions," he wrote, "to the rule that the need for identity is the most powerful and most pervasive among all species. The need for stimulation is not far behind. And security, normally, will be sacrificed for either of the other two." Then, ominously for the American welfare state he wrote, "The structure of security is the birthplace of boredom," and "Our means of satisfying innate needs are precious few, and sacrifice of any must mean replacement by another."

Mankind's requirement to feed, clothe, and shelter themselves fulfills these human needs. Work relieves boredom, and even a humdrum job brings far more stimulation than idleness. Success at a job brings status and identity that relieves anonymity. And security is by definition the result of work and labor.

Social welfare provides security, but deprives the recipient of the stimulation and identity that come from work and struggle. Writing in a biology book in the mid-sixties, almost as though he could foretell the failed future of "The Great Society," Robert Ardrey stated, "We may agree, for example, that our societies must provide greater security for the individual; yet if all we succeed in producing is a social structure providing increased anonymity and ever increasing boredom, then we should not wonder if ingenious man turns to such amusements as drugs, housebreaking, vandalism, mayhem, riots, or - at the most harmless - strange haircuts, costumes, standards of cleanliness, and sexual experiments." Nowhere else has anyone written a more apt description of the welfare predicament.

In the past 40 years, approximately four trillion dollars have been transferred to the poor. Surely a sum this vast should have made inroads against poverty. However, this four trillion dollar entitlement has been accompanied by an astronomical increase in crime, a runaway plague of alcohol and drug addiction, and a stupendous breakdown in the family unit. Billions directed at poverty have led to an astonishing increase in the numbers of poor and an explosion of street people and homeless.

Our largest and greatest city, New York, is the welfare capital of the world. Economist magazine compares life in New York to living in the middle ages or in impoverished Calcutta. In Hong Kong there is no welfare. Joblessness and poverty are hard to find in this clean and efficient city. Compare this to New York City with its vast welfare apparatus. Despite extensive government assistance, scores of homeless drug addicts and wrongdoers populate Manhattan. Segments of the city are in ruins, and some neighborhoods are blanketed with trash.

Work is part of the growth process of life. A job forces people to maintain certain standards of good character, effort, and temperance.

If you steal, lie, or take drugs while at work, you lose your job. Welfare does not weaken you as much as it excuses you from the normal pressures of employment and self sufficiency that make you stronger and improve your character.

The time is overdue for society to conclude that human nature does not harmonize with income supports. The longer people receive economic assistance the worse their social condition. Destructive behavior grows from one generation on welfare to the next. Forget racial considerations. Welfare destroys all races equally.

Bad behavior and low character are common among the welfare underclass. The media plys us with stories aimed to arouse our social sympathy for the poor. They overlook that in America today, "poor" stands as much for poor character as it does for poverty.

Many of our poor deserve far less sympathy and least of all do they deserve a check. Theirs is not the same kind of poverty that we see in Ethiopia or Bangladesh where jobs don't exist. Anybody can get a job here as millions of dirt poor immigrants of every racial background prove conclusively. There is a job within walking distance in every American city. While jobs go begging, these people refuse to work. Why work when you don"t have to? It's so easy to get a government check.

The solution is not to reform welfare. The solution is to abolish permanent subsidies altogether. Short term aid, temporary workfare, and private charities, are a few alternatives. Otherwise, the cities will continue to waste away and crime will overwhelm us.

What do subsidies and welfare have to do with gold? They are a large component of budgetary and spending excesses. They tax the court and penal system. They have a poisonous impact on the culture via subsidizing character deficiencies. They would not exist without onerous levels of taxation and the continuous inflation of money and credit.

Destruction of the money through inflating goes hand in hand with the destruction of the good character of the people; it's synonymous with more socialism and less freedom. Debase the money and you debase the culture. Said another way, the welfare system is a symptom of a monetary system that finances big government and its interventionist philosophy. Economic retrogression and failure follow whenever that strategy has been fully implemented. Adoption of this bankrupt philosophy in the U.S. represents a forceful argument for gold ownership.

CHAPTER VIII

ANECDOTAL EVIDENCE

"The fate of the nation and the fate of the currency are one and the same."

Dr. Franz Pick

"Liberals do the wrong things for the right reasons."

J. Cook

"The first requisite of a sound monetary system is that it put the least possible power over the quantity or quality of money in the hands of the politicians.

Henry Hazlitt

They dropped the boy off at my house one spring day. His mother had poisoned herself with too much whiskey. She was dead at age 41. The boy had stayed with his Mom's bleary-eyed boyfriend until the funeral was over. Now his sisters had asked if my wife and I would take him for a few days. They knew that I had sometimes taken the boy fishing. He had no Dad. His father had molested the boy's two half-sisters and then skipped town. He had never once called the boy.

The mother had always been on welfare and she'd always been a drinker. She left the boy alone every night while she sat in a bar. At age four and five he would turn all the lights on, afraid to be alone at night. She had a disability and needed crutches to get around. But she could have worked. There were plenty of suitable desk jobs. Instead the government enabled her to drink herself to death. The damage didn't end there.

Without maternal love none of us would amount to much. If a woman loves alcohol or drugs more than her children, her kids suffer for it. Often their emotions will be stunted, their character weakened and their habits irrational. They emulate the dysfunction they see and they learn to be parents unto themselves. By age five or six what ails and disturbs them may no longer be fixed.

The boy was eleven when he came to us. His sisters had lives of their own and a few days turned into a few years. He had school problems and we soon got to know a series of grade school and junior high teachers. Sometimes he seemed devoid of emotion and couldn't seem to resist any wrongdoing that might impress a classmate.

A year later I inquired at the welfare department about another child. Without thinking, I mentioned the boy who had come to live with us. They flipped out! They couldn't believe we had the boy without them knowing about it. They insisted we go through a process to see if we could qualify as foster parents. They inspected our home. I laughed. The boy had come from a hovel into an expensive home but the social worker criticized the lack of a handrail on one stairway. After wrangling awhile they gave us the boy. By that time his constant misbehaving made us unsure that we wanted him.

Another year passed and one day he stole my Suburban and went for a drive. That was the last straw. We investigated special schools and programs for delinquent boys. We found an outward bound program in Montana. We took him to see the place. We liked the school and decided he could spend the year there with thirty other disturbed kids and their counselors. It cost us $30,000 for the year.

After eight months the welfare department found out about it. They said we had no right to send him out of state. We weren't taking their money so we disagreed. They got a court order and brought him back. They stuck him in a foster home and took us to court. The judge ruled in our favor. Back went the boy to Montana. The school urged us to keep him there one more year. We agreed, but after a few months they called and said he couldn't stay any longer. He'd worn them down.

They recommended a 30-day program at a hospital in California. It cost $30,000 for the month. We had insurance and in desperation we sent him. After four weeks he came home dressed in leather, several tattoos, earrings and a minor social infection. I wrote the hospital and told them they were running a racket.

He went to live with his sister. They clashed. He moved in with a girl. At age 16 he became a father. He lived off the girlfriend's AFDC checks. They split up. She had another child with someone else. Then he got another girl pregnant with her second child. This girlfriend bought him a car with her AFDC check. It soon quit running. He needed money to buy a mobile home for his new family. I gave him the downpayment. Within a few months they lost the place. He got a job but quit after the first paycheck. Another guy moved in with them. After a few months he found them together and moved out.

He called me the other day. The first girlfriend had dropped off their daughter while she went to get something to eat. She'd been gone for three days. Now he was growing tired of baby-sitting and being a Dad. I called around and got him a couple of job interviews. He didn't make them. He's nineteen with a clouded future.. Perhaps he'll get a third girl pregnant to share the AFDC money.

You'll probably never read about the boy in the newspapers. He's not a hardened criminal like so many products of welfare. But unless something changes his life will always be a mess. Unfortunately, the government encourages him and the young girls he cohabitates with to reproduce at a breakneck pace. The more children, the more money. We tend to blame the girls but the boys also enjoy the financial rewards. Supposedly we do this for the children. But the children benefit the least.

The press likes to depict the poor as being just like the people next door but with a run of bad luck. If those writers could actually live next door to the poor they would soon quit their sympathetic stories. Twenty-five years ago I bought an apartment building in a transitional neighborhood. The Realtor lied about the tenants. The renters were of all races and they shared a common trait. They rarely paid their rent. On the outside it was a nice looking building but on the inside it was a disaster. The security company I hired to install a buzzer system on the front door quit in disgust. Every time the installer went out to his truck for a part someone stole everything he had left inside.

The tenants wrecked the apartments. They stole whatever they could. They disfigured the walls and the floors. They slept on mattresses on the floor and hung sheets over windows. They lied about the rent and they skipped out without paying. One evening I tried to collect some overdue rent. Two women were in one apartment with two cute little girls about three and four. Right in front of my eyes the mother gave each child a couple of puffs of marijuana and sent them off towards bed. I was dumbfounded. A few days later a city inspector called me to come pick up the garbage on the boulevard. Instead I called the Realtor and put the place up for sale.

We should rely on our own experience to draw conclusions about the poor. The media and the social workers don't tell it like it is. Worst of all, the people who promoted these subsidies absolutely refuse to acknowledge the consequences of their handiwork. They insist on giving more to the poor and resisting any welfare cuts. They advocate government sponsored solutions that are doomed from the start. Expensive counseling, job training, treatment programs and other billion dollar pipe-dreams won't work. If love and nurturing and good examples are replaced by abuse, indifference and bad examples, all the government programs on earth won't help these children.

Therein lies the rub. How do we resolve the greatest problem ever created by mankind? How do we overcome fierce and fanatical resistance by the left? How do we take something away from those who count on it without an explosion of crime and rioting? How do we get the politicians to sense the enormity of this problem and to act with resolve? How do we turn this shattered system around?

The best but most controversial answer is that we stop giving people money they didn't earn. That's harsh because some will suffer terrible hardships before they give up drugs and alcohol and go to work. Temporary help from private charities will help. However, no problem-free way to end these subsidies exist. But not ending them begs disaster. The quality of our life hinges on stopping the growth of crime and dependency and shoring up families and sound values. Either we terminate welfare or it will terminate us. Halfway measures will invariably succumb to political pressure, media exposure, social sympathy, bureaucratic incompetence, economic slowdowns, and complaints by the recipients.

If we don't stop welfare, public housing, subsidies and social programs that give people money, the American dream will become a nightmare. You can see a possible blueprint for America's future in the littered inner cities, the stark and lifeless reservations, the junk strewn rural shacks and the gleaming towers of the social welfare bureaucracies and government agencies. It's no place you will want to be.

CHAPTER IX

LIBERAL LEGACY

"Whom the gods would destroy, they first subsidize."

George Roche

"All of the government's monetary, economic and political power, as well as its extensive propaganda machinery, will be enlisted in a constant battle to drive down the price of gold - but in the absence of any fundamental change in the nation's monetary, fiscal, and economic direction, simply regard any major retreat in the price of gold as an unexpected buying opportunity."

Irwin A. Schiff

"If ever there was an area in which to do the exact opposite of that which government and the media urge you to do, that area is the purchasing of gold."

Robert Ringer

I turned my mud-covered Suburban onto the gravel road leading through the Indian reservation. In the back two mallards lay on a bag of decoys. They had flown into the Saskatchewan pothole I had hunted earlier that day. I planned to give them to Bird Lady. Each year I dropped off a few plump mallards for Bird Lady and her daughters.

It was close to one in the afternoon when I turned up Bird Lady's driveway. Her house sat on the top of a knoll a quarter mile off the main gravel. I passed the run-down bungalows of her daughters and pulled into the barren, weedy yard. A dozen over-sized chickens scurried away.

I walked up the porch steps and knocked on the door. No one came. I thought about Bird Lady as I waited. She had been a beautiful woman once, but the ravages of age and alcohol had withered her into a crone. I pounded louder. It quickly dawned on me that I had come too early. Bird Lady slept and she would not get up now.

I glanced at the daughters modern bungalows that had deteriorated into hovels. Rags were stuffed into holes in windows and siding. Curtains, towels and sheets covered the windows. A beat-up car sat in front of one. Neither would the daughters rise. In past years I had noted that the daughters showed signs of advanced alcoholism. Their appearance had deteriorated. They could never seem to look me in the eye and although I had tried to engage one of them in conversation her hang-dog expression revealed a deep-seated sense of inferiority. Their children were in school today. On weekends the children would be outside in the morning at unsupervised play while the elders slept. It was that way across this and every other reservation.

In all of rural America nothing is more pathetic or sad than the Indian reservations. They are laboratories for a social experiment that has destroyed the character of people who were once the most self-sufficient on earth. Never in history has an entire category of people sunk to such levels of helplessness, addiction and degradation.

Responsibility for this wretched predicament does not lie with the 7th Cavalry or the gory spectacle at Wounded Knee. It lies with modern social scientists, bureaucrats, and assorted leftists who insist on giving these people a monthly stipend that leaves them unchallenged, unmotivated and bored senseless. People grow primarily through economic struggle. Subsidies encourage the opposite of growth. They retard and shrivel human potentiality. They are an atrocity and a national disgrace.

I rolled the Suburban down the drive, away from Bird Lady and her daughters. I passed dozens of other bungalows, some occupied, some abandoned or destroyed. No cars passed me. No one would be up for several hours. I turned it over in my mind. They must go to bed close to dawn. What weird behavioral syndrome does welfare unleash that keeps these people and any others on the permanent dole up until 4 or 5 in the morning, and asleep all day? How can they raise children on such a schedule?

That's the dirty little secret in all of this welfare nonsense. The children raise themselves. The outcome of this gross neglect, where eight year olds raise three year olds, can be seen in the soaring rate of crime, abuse, addiction and social disintegration endemic to the subsidized. The little children, the innocents, the tiny ones who crave love and nurturing, get no more attention than the dog. They play outside through the day, a bag of chips for breakfast, a Pepsi and a Ho-Ho for their lunch, unsupervised and unloved.

Twenty years ago I stood in the parking lot of a restaurant in The Pas, a small community in Northern Manitoba. I was fishing with a friend and I waited outside while he used the washroom. A large bus had pulled into the lot and disgorged its passengers. The front door of the bus was open, the driver reading a newspaper. Suddenly around the corner came a small Indian boy of about four. He was dressed neatly in shorts and he was a child of such remarkable beauty that my eyes became glued to him. He walked to the bus and stood in the sunlight, looking up into the doorway, fascinated by what he saw, radiating innocence and charm. Around the corner came his father. I glanced his way but riveted my attention back on the boy. The father encouraged him to take a few steps onto the bus. It was clear the boy had never entered a bus before and this was a high adventure for him. He took a step up and then another and surveyed the interior of the bus in wonderment. As he stepped back down I stood fascinated by the angelic demeanor that had prompted this reverential episode.

His father called to him and I looked back at the man. It startled me. The father was my age. Like the boy, he too had been handsome, but too much whiskey had left heavy lines and creases in his face. His red and sunken eyes stared out from his damaged features and his curled posture spoke of intoxication. I looked back at the boy and in a moment of dread I saw what this little angel would become. I stood silently and fought the tears.

From the beginning the Indians were at a huge disadvantage. They relied on arrows, slings and snares and their utensils were of clay. The white interlopers had tools and equipment that fascinated the Indians; items they would want desperately. Imagine it; guns, traps, metal bowls and utensils, needles, cloth, axes, beads and whiskey. Some would trade furs, some would trade land. Gifts and bribes to the Indians became a way of life along the frontier. In the end they gave up their land for goods, moved to the reservations for goods and agreed to behave for goods. They made treaties which provided them with food and cash doles. The great Sioux uprising of 1863 that took the lives of over 400 Minnesota settlers flared up because of late payments of food and other broken promises. In effect, many Indians have been getting government payments for one hundred and fifty years.

Our perceptions about welfare and subsidies are shifting at warp speed. The American people have come to understand the devastating effects of welfare even as the left has hardened their views. Advocates of the current welfare disaster remain inflexible in the face of the evidence.

Welfare payments should be linked to some kind of work. ADC mothers could at least staff day care centers that attend to their own offspring. We need to insist that these people get up in the morning and accept a minimum of responsibility. Those who abuse and neglect their children should lose them. Better to build orphanages than prisons. Adoption of these innocents should be swift and simple. Interracial adoption should be encouraged.

But common sense is not so common, especially among liberals intertwined in the politics of welfare. What they have engineered puts them at risk of history's censure. The left wants to increase welfare levels, not limit them. They don't like the idea of people working for their benefits. They refuse to link parental responsibility to payments. They insist that children are best left with their parents almost without qualification. They oppose adoption and especially interracial adoption.

Once upon a time there was a simple, honest, disciplined, happy, self-sufficient tribal culture. It exists no more. The white man ruined that. However, it was not the loss of their land or the subtle imprisonment on reservations that did-in the Indians and their culture. It was the monthly checks. The dole kills the spirit and destroys character. Subsidies are behavioral poison.

Bird Lady would have been a different person had she been required to make her own way in life. She had the potential. You could see the intelligence and humor in her eyes. She liked my visits. She could have been somebody. What a waste. Yes, there are exceptions to Bird Lady. A few Indians farm and work successfully. But the mind-numbing rate of alcoholism on the reservations approaches ninety percent. A pox on all who fail to see the cause.

CHAPTER X

KILLING THE GOOSE THAT LAID THE GOLDEN EGG

"Were we to be directed from Washington when to sow and when to reap, we should soon want bread."

Thomas Jefferson

"The truth is that capitalism has not only multiplied population figures, but at the same time, improved the people's standard of living in an unprecedented way. Neither economic thinking nor historical experience suggest that any other social system could be as beneficial to the masses as capitalism. The results speak for themselves. The market economy needs no apologists and propagandists. It can apply to itself the words of Sir Christopher Wren's epitaph in St. Paul's: 'Si monumentum requiris, circumspice.' (If you seek his monument, look around.)"

Ludwig von Mises

"We are in a world of irredeemable paper money - a state of affairs unprecedented in history."

John Exter

Only the fabulous economic output of capitalism has kept America prosperous and offset the spending ravages of big government. Without American enterprise, the dollar would have long ago wound up in the waste basket. Capitalism bails out the government. It provides most of the tax money that the bureaucrats spend. It also keeps living standards high, creates jobs, wealth, and innovative products and services that offset the ravages of excessive government regulation, taxation, and spending.

Unfortunately, that is starting to change. With the exception of high-tech a long term shrinkage of corporate profits began over a decade ago. This trend spells disaster. Without profits the whole system grinds to a halt.

Politicians may bark and yap endlessly about the reasons for our economic cycles, but none truly grasps the reasons we have problems. Economic setbacks can't be corrected with a few tax and spend measures, subsidies, or meddling in markets. To maintain our economic health we need to cure the following problems:

1. Welfare benefits, unemployment benefits and other subsidy programs weaken the work force. Certain workers will sluff off, report late, miss work, or abuse chemicals if they know a government check will replace their paycheck should they be fired. The government provides incentives to goof off.

2. Our low national savings rate is, to some extent, caused by the easy availability of subsidies. People would save more if it weren't for the wide spectrum of programs from cheap loans for education to social security. Low savings means we spend more and invest less. Our social safety net helps kill savings.

3. Taxes are a penalty on progress. With higher state and local rates, taxes now eat up almost half of a worker's earnings. Individuals and corporations could invest this money far more efficiently than the government, who transfers it to ne'er-do-wells, special interests, bailouts of federally guaranteed losers, and runaway debt service.

4. The reasons that our industries often lose ground to foreign competition begins with price. They make inroads through underselling us. The main expense of any business is labor. Foreign competition enjoys lower labor costs. Our unions may crow about raising living standards and wages, but they also price companies out of the market and cause job loss.

5. Runaway government spending requires massive borrowing in the capital markets to cover big deficits. This raises interest rates and crowds out private business. Government sucks up huge amounts of capital that would otherwise be used for constructive economic growth.

6. Business invests enormous energy in complying with a blizzard of laws and regulations. Regulators are a police force intent on tripping up errant businesses, levying fines or worse. A single regulation can exterminate an entire industry. Too much of management's attention given to regulators detracts from a company's efficiency and profits.

7. Nowadays people sue at the drop of a hat. U.S. business spends too much time and money defending itself against litigation. Suits emanating from the government can paralyze a company for years. Product liability lawsuits make innovation less likely and wipe out whole segments of commerce. America desperately needs Tort Reform, but the legal professional fiercely resists any such initiative.

8. Government subsidies to certain businesses favor their success against competitors. Legal barriers to starting a business such as permits, bonds, licenses, or regulations, help big companies fend off competitors. Government intervention stifles the competition that benefits consumers.

9. Every time the government lays down a new law or changes a regulation, it has the potential for serious damage. The changes in tax laws for real estate helped set off an economic earthquake. Lawmakers and regulators blithely and carelessly make changes that carry a profound impact and throw whole segments of industry off the track.

10. The government has fostered a national ethic of getting something for nothing. This burdens business with phony lawsuits, employee theft, trumped up medical claims, insurance fraud, and an explosion of bad character. For example, generous workman compensation benefits legislated by state governments have caused an astronomical increase in disability claims for back injuries.

11. Inflation, extreme currency fluctuations, the boom and bust cycle, and dollar devaluations, all make doing business more difficult. Inflation tends to make investment in production less rewarding than other assets.

12. Business pays for all or part of health care costs, unemployment benefits, workmen's compensation insurance, product liability insurance, social security benefits, and Medicare. When you add to this, non-productive legal costs, licensing fees, property taxes, sales tax, income tax, and excise taxes, you have a thoroughbred carrying a 300 pound jockey. In other parts of the world they don't have to carry this much weight.

13. We blame other nations for outdoing us when they do their job efficiently. We blame the politicians when we are the ones who put them in office. We blame takeover artists when the easy money and credit we want for ourselves also makes it possible for them to reap windfall profits. We blame government deficits, but we still belly up to the government trough. We are a self-satisfied lot quick to blame others, but slow to face the reality that the guaranteed life we want the government to give us has and will put us deep in the hole.

The sentiments of most government employees and the multitude who enforce the rules, are fiercely anti-business. They have little or no knowledge of how the market system works, and they see business as greed driven, and profits as an evil that government should control.

This anti-business attitude proliferates in the media. Both TV and cinema portray business leaders as criminals. The press, magazine, and book publishers, are infested with writers expressing a dislike of capitalism. Churchmen reflect these same sentiments. Professors and teachers often sneer at the system that has given them the highest living standard in history.

These people don't understand wealth creation. They don't understand that profits come from meeting the needs of others by providing products and services that improve living standards. They don't realize that consumers are the rulers of the free market because their buying choices determine the success or failure of the companies competing to serve them. They are unaware that to serve one's self-interest, the capitalist must first serve the self-interest of others. This is the moral underpinning of free enterprise. But rather than notice the unassailable high moral ground of free-market capitalism, they prefer to see greed and inequality.

When influential media voices scorn the capitalist system, it turns public attitudes against business. This trend can already be seen in court rulings and various regulations that hurt business. Judges and the court system tend to be grossly anti-business. The government seems to have no qualms about moving away from free markets towards a heavily controlled marketplace where most profits go into government coffers.

These attitudes and policies are killing the goose that laid the golden egg. Without a healthy capitalist economy our spending sins will engulf us. A major depression could make the standard recessions of the past few decades look like paradise. In such a crash, gold prices could soar to the point that the yellow metal would become unaffordable for all but a nimble few.

CHAPTER XI

RUNAWAY SUBSIDIES

"Public works are not accomplished by the miraculous power of a magic wand. They are paid for by funds taken away from the citizens."

Ludwig von Mises

"No other commodity enjoys as much universal acceptability and marketability as gold."

Hans F. Sennholz

"Of all the contrivances for cheating the laboring classes of mankind, none has been more effective than that which deludes them with paper money."

Daniel Webster

When the president and Congress do something like extend unemployment benefits, no thought is given to the budget deficit. People are going to suffer, and the pain has to be alleviated no matter what the cost. Human suffering must be remedied by the government. This view is incompatible with balancing budgets and cutting deficits. The number of grave problems in the U.S. is endless, and human suffering of one sort or another limitless.

This liberal viewpoint means that budget cutting will always be sacrificed for expensive problem solving and high priced compassion. Liberal empathy usually means spending someone else's money, and lots of it. This blind social sympathy leads to runaway spending. Forget about permanently cutting the deficit in modern America. Even with a fiscally conservative Congress, it's not going to happen in any meaningful way.

But wait a minute; What kind of a hardhearted scrooge would be against extending unemployment benefits? The answer is simple: almost any employer who studies the results. When you have secretaries quit to take the summer off and collect unemployment; when you have people leave a perfectly good job after one day and request that it not have any effect on their unemployment benefits; when job applicants tell you they have been waiting around until their benefits expire before looking for a job, you get cynical about unemployment benefits. Especially so when you have to make monthly contributions to the upkeep of people who would otherwise be getting up in the morning to look for a job.

Of course there are plenty of people to whom job loss means legitimate hardship. Without work they will suffer. But struggle is part of life. Suffering will always exist in one form or the other, and government can never cure it, only change it into another form.

No one escapes the struggles of life. Emerson tells us, "There is always some leveling circumstance that puts down the overbearing, the strong, the rich, the fortunate..." Furthermore, suffering and struggle lead directly to strength and growth. Napoleon Hill teaches, "The necessity for struggle is one of the clever devices through which nature forces individuals to expand, develop, progress and become strong....We are forced to recognize that this great universal necessity for struggle must have a definite and useful purpose. That purpose is to force the individual to sharpen his wits, arouse his enthusiasm, build up his spirit of faith, gain definiteness of purpose, develop his power of will, inspire his faculty of imagination....Meet struggle and master it, says nature, and you shall have strength and wisdom sufficient for all your needs."

In other words, this bleak period when someone loses their job should not be a time when government jumps in with a check. It should be a time when that person is forced to become self-reliant, tougher, smarter and stronger. This is a time for ingenuity, creativity, inspiration and resourcefulness. Emerson said, "When man is pushed, tormented, defeated, he has a chance to learn something, he has been put on his wits....he has gained facts; learns his ignorance, is cured of the insanity of conceit; has got moderation and real skill."

Napoleon Hill summarizes how nature's laws work in times of trouble "Suffering through physical or mental pain, disappointments' frustrations, and sorrows, is the means by which one may become great or go down in permanent failure."

What did people do a hundred years ago when there were no government give-aways? For one thing, they saved for a rainy day. Private charity helped the worst cases. Our ancestors had no government help but they got along just fine. For most of us today, a private insurance program that provided 60 or 90 days of jobless benefits would more than suffice. Instead, we have built a disgraceful spending program with incentives that foster unsavory behavior.

These unemployment doles bring about subtle changes in the attitudes of the work force. Jobs are no longer as valuable. People don't work as hard to keep them, and employers experience slightly diminished effort and increases in laziness, job turnover, and tardiness. All these negative factors effect quality, productivity, training and motivation.

Unemployment benefits are a detriment to society. They open the door to the pathway of dependence. They lure the frightened and worried into the psychological acceptance of permanent unemployment and welfare. They encourage shiftlessness, cheating, cowardice, and fear. Said Hill, "When any individual reconciles himself to the state of mind wherein he is willing to accept largess from the government instead of supplying his needs through personal initiative, that individual is on the road to decay and spiritual blindness."

These views are nowadays considered to be quaint and old fashioned. Imagine anyone arguing to abolish unemployment. However, if we are to survive as a nation, the whole welfare boondoggle must be tossed overboard. Every food stamp, energy credit, low cost loan, rent subsidy, unemployment check, and free everything else must be trashed. Something for nothing is the root of all evil in our political system. Nothing else can poison our culture, corrupt our society or ruin the character of our people like unearned money or unearned opportunity. Ultimately it will plunge us into a level of despair, wretchedness, and barbarism that we cannot currently imagine. Even gold will not make life bearable in ruined cities comprised of weaklings, malingerers, moochers, addicts and criminals.

CHAPTER XII

ECONOMIC DECLINE

"If you don't trust gold, do you trust the logic of taking a beautiful pine tree, worth about $4,000 - $5,000, cutting it up, turning it into pulp and then paper, putting some ink on it and then calling it one billion dollars?"

Kenneth J. Gerbino

"It is important to remember that government interference always means either violent action or the threat of such action. ....taxes are paid because the taxpayers are afraid of offering resistance to the tax gatherers. They know that any disobedience or resistance is hopeless. As long as this is the state of affairs, the government is able to collect the money that it wants to spend. Government is in the last resort the employer of armed men, of policemen, gendarmes, soldiers, prison guards, and hangmen. The essential feature of government is the enforcement of its decrees by beating, killing, and imprisoning. Those who are asking for more government interference are asking ultimately for more compulsion and less freedom."

Ludwig von Mises

"Borrowers will default. Markets will collapse. Gold (the ultimate form of safe money) will skyrocket."

Michael Belkin

Many people hear financial warnings these days but ignore or discount them. Economic and social deterioration takes place slowly. Sometimes this process is hard to notice. If we focus on the shocking changes in America over the past decade, however, we can get a better picture of our decline. For example, only 20 years ago, Savings and Loans were a bedrock institution built on public thrift and sound lending practices. Now they have fallen into shocking decline. If two decades ago anyone would have predicted the collapse of these savings banks they would have been laughed out of town.

Over the past decade, America has become a debtor nation. Not long ago foreigners owed us. Now we owe them. The amount of this debt grows relentlessly and reflects serious deterioration.

Two decades ago the American farmer enjoyed financial independence and a level of productivity that made agricultural exports an important leg of the economy. Today many farmers survive only because of government subsidies. Gross intervention by the government in agricultural markets led to overproduction, low prices and falling land values. Nowadays a farmer can get paid for producing on half his land, and also be paid for not producing on the other half.

In the past decade, every major U.S. city has become a nightmare of violence and drug addiction. Prisons are sprouting up around the country to hold a swelling population of criminals. Unsafe city streets in major population centers swarm with addicts, lunatics, and muggers. Not long ago public schools had to worry about gum chewing and tardiness. Now they must cope with armed students, drug dealing, vandalism, and murder.

Even more ominous is the burden of rising debt levels for consumers and corporations. Corporate and personal bankruptcy are at an all time high. Meanwhile the promotion of easy to get loans, second mortages, home refinancings, credit cards and margin loans has reached epidemic proportions. This trailblazing expansion of credit raises questions about deteriorating credit standards to say nothing of prudence.

Unquestionably, America is beginning to fail. Most of our social and economic problems did not even exist ten or twenty years ago. A search for the culprit invariably reveals the heavy hand of government. Excessive levels of government spending, borrowing, and regulation burden the market system, impair the economy, and promise to eventually ruin the value of the dollar.

Government solutions make the cure worse than the problem. For example, two of the government's greatest initiatives have been the elimination of poverty and racial prejudice. Despite these efforts and undoubtedly because of them, poverty levels have deteriorated and race relations are worse than ever. The national prayer should read, "Lord, please deliver us from the government trying to solve any more of our problems."

America's moral foundation has turned to quicksand. Initially this country stressed individual freedom, self-reliance, limited government, low taxes, and the sound ethics of a Yankee merchant. Under today's morality you are "entitled" to get a piece of what someone else worked for. In this century an absurdly large government functions principally to extract money from those who earned it, in order to give it to those who didn't.

Can you justify taking someone's money simply because another person may be in need of it? What moral right does anyone have to someone else's earnings? At least Robin Hood stole from the corrupt. The U.S. government goes right after the hardest working citizens, the most productive, and the most talented, and picks their pockets. Those that provide the new jobs, innovative products, and who please consumers the most, are victimized by the state and its hoard of tax collectors.

If you are robbed at gunpoint in a New York alley and your money is handed out to a group of homeless huddled in the street, does that make the robbery okay? That's the moral justification of the government's redistribution policy. Furthermore, if you don't pay them on time, someone will come from the government to enforce their demands. They will resort to force, wave a gun in your face, handcuff you, and throw you in jail. Then they will sell off your worldly possessions and give the proceeds to someone who refuses to work. But only after they first take a big cut to pay themselves.

We shouldn't be puzzled that no good comes from this dubious moral system. The chief cause of America's decline is rooted in the moral rot of redistribution. No long term benefit can ever come from this corrupt practice, only social disintegration.

We are in decline because we have changed the sound policies that built the country. No income tax levies hampered the great entrepreneurs who built American industry. They kept their profits and plowed them back, multiplying productivity. Imagine the enormous penalty inflicted on industry today when so much capital goes to Federal, State and local governments. The larger the government, the larger its appetite and the more it spends. Government has turned into a dispensor of spoils.

A hundred years ago corporate and personal taxes were low or nonexistent. Government spending programs changed this. From decade to decade, taxes rose endlessly. Government became a parasite on the productive sector. Money nourishes this monster and makes him greedy for more. That's why taxes keep going higher over the long term. Once the tax genie is out of the bottle, the plundering of the productive knows no limit.

Not satisfied with merely bleeding the industrious, the government spends more than can be extracted through taxation.The government's annual budget creeps into the red, a little initially, then more, as bulging beneficiaries of new programs belly up to the government trough. Before long, the government spends money recklessly on grants and subsidies, always growing, squandering and funding worse than useless projects. Red ink rises. Deficits become a problem, then a disaster. In time, this spending spins out of control.

Government gives handouts to millions of recipients who are transformed into raging malcontents, screaming for more. The ever worsening consequences of pork-barrel politics and pushy special interest groups must ultimately lead to economic distortions, inflation, and recession. That's the inevitable payoff for runaway taxation and redistribution.

To fund this spending mayhem, the government must enlist the Federal Reserve to aid in a process of currency debasement. They create money from thin air with bookkeeping entries in the amount they can't squeeze from the taxpayer. This inflation causes the public's money in banks to lose value. This subtle form of taxation reduces the buying power of all money in circulation. It's a form of cheating. If they can't tax away your savings, they dilute them through the creation of new money (Inflating). Or they keep interest rates artificially low to encourage borrowing and consumption. That's why we have the current enormous debt buildup.

The government taxes all it can, prints all it can, and finally borrows all it can. This chicanery weakens the nations financial institutions (the S & L's, banks and insurance companies). The government then offers its own safe harbor, by backing its T-bills, notes, and bonds with the full credit of the government. This gives them the inside track on borrowing. Unfortunately their swollen demands can wreak havoc in the capital markets and sometimes squeeze out private borrowers.

Until this ongoing government expansion and currency debasement ends, gold should be an important part of any investment strategy. In fact, gold may be critically important for many years into the future. Because current trends aren't likely to turn around, gold will be the best way to hedge against these government actions.

A booming stock market temporatily glosses over over many of the setbacks and sins in our society. These come to light and become unmanageable at the end of a boom. In tough times we pay for our crimes.

People want prosperity to continue. They don't want to hear bad news that rocks the boat. They want their investment gains intact and their mutual funds rising. How can anything be wrong in a country where 25% a year is the norm? How can we fault a goverment that's close to balancing the budget? Unfortunately, this temporary good news cloaks deep stuctural problems in the economy and the currency.

CHAPTER XIII

DECADE OF CRISIS

"The international monetary order is more precarious by far today than it was in 1929. Then, gold was international money, incorruptible, unmanageable, and unchangeable. Today, the U.S. dollar serves as the international medium of exchange, managed by Washington politicians and Federal Reserve officials, manipulated from day to day, and serving political goals and ambitions. This difference alone sounds the alarm to all perceptive observers."

Hans F. Sennholz

"Deficit spending is simply a scheme for the 'hidden' confiscation of wealth. Gold stands in the way of this insidious process. It stands as a protector of property rights."

Alan Greenspan

"Politicians can't give us anything without depriving us of something else. Government is not a god. Every dime they spend must first be taken from someone else."

Barry Asmus

In conjunction with the broad-based economic and social decline of America, the financial markets will someday join the collapse. The insidious growth of government and its direct relationship to our decline and fall are the national blind spot. A pending financial crash may reveal the extent of our decay.

The politicians and the media can trivialize the erosion of the dollar in foreign exchange markets. However, a nation's currency speaks volumes about its affairs. A decade ago 260 yen bought a dollar - today it's less than 130 yen. That's a drastic reduction in value in just 10 years. Over the long term the once mighty dollar is failing. If our currency collapses the country can't be far behind.

The reason our dollar is periodically in trouble is no secret. We don't save and invest as we once did. We borrow, spend and consume. We buy so much overseas they choke on our dollars. Our recent economic recovery did not originate with plant expansion and renewed commercial construction. Instead it came from refinanced mortgage money, credit cards and loans that were spent on new cars and trips to the mall. Our economic health improved because we ate out more and charged more.

The consumer debt buildup eventually cuts into future consumer spending. This debt slows the economy when consumers must pay back principal and interest.

Corporations also struggle under their repayment burden. If interest rates rise as the economy slows, corporate profits diminish and substantial layoffs swell the unemployment rate. These events foster further weakness in consumer income. Consumers buy less. Corporate profits suffer further. Layoffs and job losses mount, setting off a further downward spiral. Too much debt is one of the many factors that can create an economic crash.

Economist Kurt Richebacher explains other reasons for a bust, "Driven by an overborrowing and dissaving consumer and a capital spending boom narrowly based on high tech, the U.S. economy's strength is definitely precarious and illfounded. It is bubble-strength that tends to deflate like a punctured tire."

"The U.S. is actually experiencing the most dramatic inflation in its history. But the inflation in the U.S. is of the worst kind. It is rampant asset inflation, the same brand that led to the deflationary collapse of Japan and the Tiger economies. The principal difference is that, in the U.S. the asset bubble is translating into unsustainable overconsumption."

"We have long since given up looking for rationality in the stock market. This is especially so now, when the whole world financial community is addicted to speculation as never before in history.

"The chief risk factor both for the U.S. stock market and the U.S. economy is the impending sharp earnings slowdown. This will finally shatter the prevailing hype and, in sequence, puncture first the stock market bubble , second the spending bubble, and third the dollar bubble. A serious bear market would cause recession. Full-blown deflation cannot and will not come in the U.S. until the stock market crashes, but the crash is only a matter of time."

"Central banks keep their money spigots wide open. What we are witnessing is the bursting of a global credit and asset bubble that has created unprecedented global imbalances and indebtedness and absurdly overvalued stock markets. These wildly speculative markets are unpredictable in the short run, but the thing to see is that the risks on the downside grossly outweigh the remaining mini-potential on the upside."

"Financial speculation (creating merely psuedo wealth) has replaced productive investment, which alone creates real wealth. In contrast to the rampant euphoria in financial markets, the capitalistic ecomomies are in a relentless demise."

Here are the major trends in the U.S. that argue for a collapse:

1. The national savings rate is woeful.

2. Profits are in a long-term decline.

3. The capital investment rate has fallen to an insufficient level.

4. Incomes continue to fall - down 6% in the past few years.

5. Corporate downsizing and restructuring go on unabated.

6. The dollar falls unremittingly over the long term.

7. Overconsumption of imports permanently balloons the balance of payment deficit.

8. Productivity falls.

9. Speculation runs rampant.

10. Leveraging grows relentlessly.

11. Fiat money creation never stops and inflation constantly lurks in the wings.

12. Government spending continues to expand.

13. Chronic budget deficits fall but still balloon the national debt.

14. Government bureaucracy grows despite cuts.

15. The cost of government guarantees, spending commitments and future promises defy computation.

16. Crime flattens out at a high level.

17. Illegitimacy soars.

18. Dependency on government subsidies steadily expands.

19. Politics infiltrates every aspect of the government's activities.

20. Government interference in commerce grows.

21. Litigation soars and government lawsuits in newly legislated areas become increasingly irrational.

22. Reasonable environmentalism disintegrates into extremism and hostility to progress.

23. Political correctness takes root and flourishes in institutions of higher learning.

24. Leading universities graduate increasing numbers of students hostile to America and contemptuous of its history.

25. A growing intellectual class loathes capitalism and disparages the nation's bedrock institutions of family, religion, and personal responsibility.

26. Entertainment and media echo the anti-capitalist and statist sentiments of the left.

27. The leadership of American churches drifts ever leftward.

What are the long-term consequences of these trends for gold?The Global Gold Stock Report predicts, "Without hesitation, I tell you that within ten years, perhaps sooner, gold will be remonetized. All the major world currencies will be backed by gold or they will not be accepted as payment of any debt except internally, within the country of issue. The world is on the verge of a financial upheaval, and the forces for change have been building for decades. It will happen, and when it does it will be swift. Watch the dollar closely. The value of the dollar will continue to decline against other world currencies, and this decline will accelerate. No one will want to be left holding dollars that are losing value daily, and this will only add fuel to the fire. Inflation will grow at an alarming rate, and interest rates will sky-rocket. The U.S. Government will not be able to come to its own rescue, as it will be obvious to the world there is no possible way for the Government to ever pay off its debt. This is the reality. It is inevitable. This same scenario has been played time and time again in many countries: Germany, Argentina, Austria, Bolivia, and Brazil are just a few examples."

If they are true, these predictions of an increased reliance on gold are a secondary consequence of big government and its left-leaning policies. The primary consequences are a deteriorating economic performance and social decay. We don't know how bad things can become, but the potential exists for a new kind of dark ages where economic pain aggravates social unrest, and anarchy and misery threaten order. We are all victims of a fatal leftist error. Liberals never analyze the consequences of their simplistic government solutions. They believe that if government pours money on a problem that it will cure it. But as an age-old proverb tells us, "For everything that is given, something is taken." Emerson stated it neatly, "Everything has its price - and if that price is not paid, not that thing but something else is obtained....it is impossible to get anything without its price."

This simple rule of life and nature is the Achilles' heel of collectivism, socialism, and modern liberalism. It explains why government programs so often bear bitter fruit. Rather than acknowledge the sorry results of the programs they promote, the left puts a different spin on the facts and defends their false conclusions with statistical fraud. In this dogmatic refusal to see real-life consequences, they differ little from the superstitious priesthood of ancient Egypt.

Liberal true-believers are convinced that government must solve the problems of society because no one else can. The fact that government does it so poorly matters not. They refuse to see that government initiatives exhaust the resources of the country and corrupt the citizenry. Unfortunately, their view that government can micro-manage the affairs of the people is the death knell for order and prosperity.

The economic woes of the U.S. are so serious that massive stimulation of some kind must take place to try and keep the economy from collapsing. In reality, the U.S. should take its medicine, suffer through the downturn and stop credit and debt expansion. This won't happen. The country won't take the pain voluntarily. Rather, it will be forced upon us by events that suddenly spin out of control. Gold will be the best asset to own in such an environment.

CHAPTER XIV

A TRILLION HERE, A TRILLION THERE

"An examination of the finances of other government-backed agencies indicates that the S&L bail out may be just the tip of the fiscal iceberg about to strike the American taxpayer."

Ronald Utt, The Heritage Foundation

"...the gold standard, in one form or another, will prevail long after the present rash of national fiats is forgotten or remembered only in currency museums."

Hans F. Sennholz

"Increasingly, the wealth of the modern world has come to be represented by financial assets rather than real assets, and this to me is a very unhealthy situation, because financial assets are inherently unstable. Financial assets (currencies, bonds, mortgages, stocks, bank credit, etc.) can be quickly and violently reduced in value, or destroyed completely by either inflation or deflation."

Donald J. Hoppe

In the harsh depression of the 1930's personal and corporate debt were less significant than they are today. The government was not on the hook as a guarantor for trillions of dollars. Government guarantees will be in the news time and again in the 1990's, and could well be the crisis that forces a currency debasement and the doom of the dollar.

A shocking report from the Heritage Foundation warned that the $150 and $300 billion that was required to bail out the S&L's is but the tip of the iceberg! Trillions more may be required to prop up the financial obligations of numerous other government agencies. According to the report, "The government's total risk exposure of nearly $6 trillion is more than twice the national debt and more than five times the annual federal budget—and much of that obligation is in bad shape."

Several trillion dollars of the obligations are linked directly to the financial health of real estate. Rounded off to the nearest half-trillion they include:

$1 Trillion - S&L Deposit Insurance

$2 Trillion - Federal Deposit Insurance

$1/2 Trillion - VA & FHA Mortgages

$1/2 Trillion - FNMA, FMHA, etc.

Heritage further stated, "Default rates in many of the government direct loan and loan guarantee programs are rising at an alarming rate and could lead to huge losses which will have to be met by the taxpayer. The FDIC and the FHA posted their first-ever losses in 1988 and repeated that performance in 1989. With the residential and commercial real estate markets still weak, this trend could continue through 1990." (Editors note: this report was issued early in this decade. All the numbers are no doubt much larger now.)

Problems in the real estate market and the emerging problems with $6 trillion of financial obligations underwritten by the government are all parts of a worrisome financial picture that is gradually gaining attention. For example, a recent letter written to Congress by the Business Roundtable, a prestigious group of business leaders, had this to say, "In the brief period of the past decade, we have amassed trillions of dollars of debt; we have regressed from being the largest creditor nation in the world to the biggest debtor; we have witnessed the federal deficit absorb over half our net private savings; we have become increasingly dependent upon foreign capital, inexorably ceding our influence over both our domestic and international policies. And we have embarked upon a course which cannot be sustained without high costs—economic, social, and human."

Michael Aronstein, of Comstock Partners, warned in a Barron's Weekly interview:

"The natural cyclicality of the economy, cycles of exuberance and depression, has been completely overridden by the government's indemnification of the whole financial sector. Which means you can't have small accidents any more.

"There are all these artificial, risk-avoidance statutes on the books. They have a whole mythology of riskless finance: Don't worry, this is too big to fail. The government will prevent this from happening. Nobody has ever lost money in an insured deposit. Nobody has ever lost money in a money-market fund because theFed would never permit it. All of this nonsense was based on the assumption that the reckless deployment of credit can be glossed over by government's willingness to step in and utilize its credit rating.

"And at some point there will be an admission of the inability of government to live up to its financial promises. Not in terms of sustaining people's income, but of guaranteeing the value of all these financial assets that it guarantees.

"We are about to discover that all of these promises made by government pertaining to finance are empty.

"Government is having to back away from more and more of its promises. Whether it is a promise to keep the streets safe or the promise to try and give every kid a decent, safe education—whatever, they can't meet these promises.

"All these promises about retirement will be broken. You know, if you work for your 35 years you can retire comfortably and the next generation will pay for it through Social Security. And you can have your bank deposits earn high interest with no risk because they'll pay for it if your bank does something silly. And they will insure everybody's medical care. All these promises will be broken.

"We have got a society that is promoting this mythology that nobody is even going to get a hangnail, no matter how irresponsibly they behave in the financial sector. And it is nonsense. It is a great pandemic delusion, and it is unfortunate because it is ruining the best country in the world."

How will all of this effect the U.S. currency? According to a leading German banker, Walter Seipp, U.S. dominance of global finance will decline and the U.S. dollar will no longer be the major international currency. He warns, "The U.S. cannot go on as it is at present. The net external debts it would have accumulated...mean that its interest burden would no longer be bearable. Moreover it's unlikely that the capital flows from abroad—i.e., investments from Japan or Europe—will continue during the 1990's." He concludes that the dollar will be hard pressed to maintain its position because the currency has, "far more weight than is indicated by the economic and financial significance of the U.S. Its relative decline is fairly certain."

Should this happen, and we are suggesting that it will, the price of gold will rise to much higher levels. Not even the mighty U.S. government can borrow, guarantee, and subsidize its way into prosperity. The greater the mortgage placed on our future, the greater the extent of our ultimate decline. The ceiling has not caved in yet, but the cracks are clearly visible to all who wish to see them.

CHAPTER XV

ENVY

"It is a socialist idea that making profits is a vice. I consider that the real vice is making losses."

Winston Churchill

"All previous attempts to base money solely on intangibles such as credit or government edict or fiat have ended in inflationary panic and disaster."

Donald Hoppe

"There can be no other criterion, no other standard than gold. Yes, gold which never changes, which can be shaped into ingots, bars, coins, which has no nationality and which is eternally and universally accepted as the unalterable fiduciary value par excellence."

Charles De Gaulle

Scratch a socialist or liberal and you'll find a person who's worried about someone else making a profit or high income. Why is that? Envy partially explains these sentiments. Author Helmut Schoek writes, "Envy is a drive which lies at the core of man's life as a social being..." In America the politics of envy can get you elected to the highest office in the land.

Against the backdrop of envy, Capitalism does not fare well. According to the Austrian economist, Ludwig von Mises, capitalism rewards those who bring products and services to the market that contribute most to the well being of the people. Under this system the consumers are supreme. Wealth can only be acquired by serving consumers. The buying choices of the people decide who succeeds and who fails. Under Capitalism, everyone has the opportunity to become an entrepreneur or attain a profession or position that pays off handsomely. However, this system allows no excuses for personal shortcomings or failure.

Many self-made people started from the same place as others who failed or who did not forge ahead. The sight of people who have given proof of greater ability bothers some people. To console themselves they rationalize that their skills have gone unrecognized. They blame capitalism, which they claim does not reward the meritorious but gives the prize to dishonest businesses, greedy speculators, crooked entrepreneurs, and other exploiters. They were too honest to swindle people, and they chose virtue over riches.

In a society where everyone is the founder of his or her own fortune, it is particularly galling to the teacher, the politician, the artist, or the bureaucrat, to see the large income disparity between themselves and successful entrepreneurs. That's why they advocate socialism, which promises to level incomes and allows the state to control economic outcomes.

These complainers have the same opportunity as everyone else to meet the needs and wants of the public with a better or cheaper product. However, if they prefer writing philosophical texts or poetry they can't make as much money as someone who satisfies the needs and wants of a greater number of people. That is the law of the market. Those who satisfy the wants of a smaller number of people collect fewer consumer buying choices or dollars than those who satisfy the majority of people. In money-making, the creator of computer software outstrips the social critic or the sculptor. Under capitalism, everybody's station in life depends on their own doing.

Even among many conservatives there exists an unhealthy level of hatred towards the wealthy. Nor do they hesitate to join with professors and politicians to suggest that the worst exploitation and greed comes from big business. They fail to realize that large corporations got that way because they did a superior job of meeting the product needs of the people in the best and cheapest way.

The hallmark of big business is mass production for the benefit of the masses. In fact, big business standardizes the people's ways of consumption and enjoyment, and every citizen shares in most of these material blessings.

Nobody goes without in the market economy because someone got rich. The money earned by the rich is not the cause of anyone's poverty. The same process that makes people rich satisfies people's wants and needs. The most millionaires are found in countries with the highest living standards. The entrepreneurs and the capitalists prosper only to the extent that they succeed in supplying and satisfying the consumer.

The glaring misunderstanding of capitalism and how it works in our society originates more from envy than intellect. This mix of envy and ignorance explains everything from the inroads of Lenin to the socialists who have led us down the path to fewer freedoms and more government. The same anti-capitalist sentiment exists today among the so-called intellectuals and their liberal bedfellows who infest our government. As always, they promote a detrimental socialist philosophy. While the rest of the world moves towards capitalism and prosperity, we are stuck with big government. As the playwright George Bernard Shaw said, "You have to choose (as a voter) between trusting to the natural stability of gold and the natural stability and intelligence of the members of the government. And with due respect to these gentlemen, I advise you, as long as the capitalist system lasts, to vote for gold."

CHAPTER XVI

THE FREEDOM PHILOSOPHER

"Betting against gold is the same as betting on governments. He who bets on governments and government money bets against 6,000 years of recorded human history."

Gary North

"Gold is forever. It is beautiful, useful, and never wears out. Small wonder that gold has been prized over all else, in all ages, as a store of value that will survive the travails of life and the ravages of time."

James Blakeley

"The proper and limited use of government is to invoke a common justice and keep the peace - and that is all."

Leonard Read

If Ludwig von Mises gave body to the economics of freedom, then his friend and contemporary, Leonard Read gave it spirit. Leonard Read founded the "Foundation for Economic Education". He wrote 29 books. In his biography, Mary Sennholz wrote that he "....rallied the demoralized and tired forces of individual freedom..."

Writing in 1946, Leonard Read warned about the inroads of government...."more and more people are coming to believe that the free market should be shelved and that, in its stead, government should use its police force to take the income of some and give it.....to the government's idea of the needy." In other words, from each according to his effort, to each according to his lack of effort.

A half century ago Read could write, "Socialistic practices are now so ingrained in our thinking, so customary, so much a part of our mores, that we take them for granted." Today's scope and size of public housing, Medicare and government subsidies dwarfs anything in Leonard Read's time. He, I'm sure, would argue that we have embraced socialism all the more.

One sign of the damaging effect of these subsidies shows up in elections. Joseph Sobran aptly describes the reason liberals win. "Voters who live off taxpayers are the Democrats' ace in the hole. The Democrats created the big programs and never let the recipients forget it. This gives them an initial advantage of tens of millions of votes in any presidential election."

Leonard Read held these vote-buying government programs in contempt. He wrote, "... statism is but socialized dishonesty; it is feathering the nests of some with feathers coercively plucked from others - on the grand scale. There is no moral difference between the act of a pickpocket and the progressive income tax or any other social program." He explained, "That there is no greater dishonesty than man effecting his own private gains at the expense of others." Read argued, "That the practice of dishonesty is evil and that retribution follows the doing of evil. Every evil act commits us to its retribution."

Leonard Read asks, "Is the extortion of your income (in order that another may have the say-so as to what it will be spent for) a creative act?" His answer, "Extortion - coercion - is destructive. It destroys your freedom of choice! Coercion, by its nature, is destructive." (In this context coercion means forcing a citizen to do what he or she would not do if left to their own devices.) He quotes Frederic Bastiat as the litmus test on whether a government action is aggressive or violent. "See if the law takes from some persons what belongs to them, and gives it to other persons to whom it does not belong."

Because of government coercion a trickle of people are beginning to leave the U.S. Some leave to escape the high taxes. Others resent the degree of government intrusion. These libertarians are searching the world over for comfortable climates, amenities and maximum freedom. Others consider leaving because they are horrified by the results of government programs that foster crime and bad character. They look for crime-free zones within and without the U.S.

Towards the end of the Roman Empire its citizens began to leave Rome (300 AD). They preferred to live with the barbarians. It was the only way to escape exorbitant taxes, mobs of poor clamoring for government handouts and heavy handed bureaucrats strangling private business. We haven't quite come to that yet, but present trends of redistribution ultimately spell disaster. The policies of the liberals and socialists are the prescription for national suicide.

Leonard Read argued that income redistribution harms everyone involved in the process, starting with the person whose property or assets are taken. It discourages private charity, "that kindly sentiment and conduct which strengthens the bonds of a common brotherhood." Read saw voluntary charity as a highly important attribute of society and decried its decline. He complained, "The state will practice charity for you. A common brotherhood, by some quirk of reasoning, is to become a collective act of compulsion!" He also saw enormous economic damage. Savings (now taxed off) would otherwise have been invested in (tools, machinery and factories) to create jobs, wealth and greater financial security.

Of the person in need Leonard Read writes, "Does any able adult person 'in need' really benefit by living on the confiscated income of others? Does this ever improve his character or his mental and physical faculties? His growth? Does anyone ever benefit by the removal of self-responsibility?" He adds "To live on loot appears to be no further removed from evil than to take the loot." It should be plain to see "that the evil means of confiscating income must lead to an evil end to those who live on it."

Of the bureaucrats who tax and enforce Leonard Read wrote, "I cannot indulge in my own upgrading at the same time I am inhibiting someone else's creative action. Therefore, to the extent that one's life is spent in using force to coerce others, to that extent is one's life destroyed and its higher purpose frustrated."

Leonard Read knew that the absence of government intrusion was responsible for the great burst of creativity that lifted our country to its exalted economic position. He wrote, "The Constitution and the Bill of Rights more severely limited government than government had ever before been limited." Two benefits occurred. "...individuals did not turn to government for security, welfare, or prosperity because government was so limited that it had little on hand to dispense..." and this limited power did not "permit taking from some citizens and giving to others."

So, "The American people gained a world-wide reputation for being self-reliant." And since the government did not much interfere, tax away income or force people to do what they otherwise wouldn't do, "there was a freeing, a releasing of creative energy on a scale unheard of before." Excessive government (Socialism) intimidates and discourages this process. Says Read, "Nothing creative is induced by compulsion." In other words, "Law and decree cannot serve as a creative force, any more than can a gun."

The Soviets showed us how sterile and destructive to human creativity is Socialism. They survived on what they stole, borrowed or copied because "Socialism depends upon.....material achievements which socialism itself can never create." This is the definition of a parasite. "Socialism takes and redistributes wealth, but it is utterly incapable of creating wealth." In other words, social programs detract from our prosperity.

Leonard Read further warned, "Man cannot feign the role of

God without finally playing the devil's part." Is there any better example of this than in the socialist Russia of Lenin and Stalin? Through the horrible deeds and consequences of collectivist actions we can see clearly "that man playing God is a prime evil, an evil seed that must grow to a destructive bloom, however pretty it may appear in its earlier stages."

Read wrote, "that we cannot maintain the present degree of statism, let alone drive further toward the omnipotent state, without our great economy flying to pieces." He warned of this peril decades ago. Yet he has passed from the scene and no serious collapse occurred. Why then haven't we seen a crash? How have we avoided a crisis? The answer: inflation. We take larger and larger doses of financial narcotics to forestall pain.

As I've said, inflation means diluting the means of exchange through increasing the money supply. Says Read, "Inflation makes the extension of socialism possible by providing the financial chaos in which it flourishes. The fact is that socialism and inflation are simultaneously cause and effect; they feed on each other!"

Inflation also keeps the financial markets rising. New money funnels into speculation, leveraging, borrowing and refinancing. It lubricates a vast credit and debt expansion, encouraging consumers to borrow to the hilt, thereby feeding a consumption boom that keeps the economy humming. Inflating provides short-term bliss while monstrous balance of payment deficits, reliance on foreign lenders, low capital formation, meager savings, faltering productivity, and high levels of public and private debt chronicle the insidious works of socialism.

That's what our whole government edifice is - Socialism, a word less and less used to describe what's happening more and more. Social Security, unemployment compensation, Medicare, public housing, welfare benefits, Medicaid, agricultural subsidies, school loans - you name it - it's Socialism. The use of the socialist label has become old-fashioned and quaint, branding the person who uses the term as a reactionary out of step with modern trends. Sorry. Ultimately, all of these increasingly expensive social programs are going to fail and disappear. What you subsidize you get more of until the costs become unaffordable and the program is cut back until it's unrecognizable or abolished

Socialism kills progress, destroys creativity, smothers freedom, chokes off productivity and bleeds the citizens dry. It bankrupts nations. It has hidden its sorry results by lurking behind mountains of debt and by slowly ruining the currency through inflation. When its dirty work is finally exposed, the economy will be ruined, the markets in a shambles, the currency debased and the people in shock. A wise man said, "Ultimately with God's aid, Truth always emerges and finally prevails supreme in its power over the destiny of mankind, and terrible is the retribution for those who deny, defy, or betray it."

This crash I write about will not be postponed indefinitely. The single best historic indicator of economic collapse and shrinking prosperity has been unprecedented extremes in debt, speculation, real estate values, consumption, leverage, stock values and social trends. It is these excesses that can turn normal corrections into panics because the margins for error have been eroded by excessive optimism, greed and arrogance.

The refusal to see the enormity of the current excesses and to ignore the sorry historical record of panics and crashes is in itself a sign of trouble ahead. It's quite possible that this nearsighted nation stands on the precipice of a historic collapse. The wealth of the American people is at risk.

CHAPTER XVII

THE ROLE OF GOLD

"Gold is not going to fade away and just become another useful metal."

Donald Hoppe

"Never have the world's moneys been so long cut off from their metallic roots."

Murray M Rothbard

"The gold standard sooner or later will return with the force and inevitability of natural law, for it is the money of freedom and honesty."

Hans F. Sennholz

Only a few commodities have true worldwide followings. The widespread international market for gold provides a degree of liquidity that renders gold less susceptible to any single nation's financial problems. That's why gold may be impervious to the same kinds of market drops that can affect stocks and other assets. Stock markets are national and go up and down based on a nation's investment mood and economic performance.

Gold doesn't bear interest because gold represents capital that's not at risk. It can't be affected by a bank failure, a market crash or a corporate bankruptcy. It can be argued that buying gold for possession in a relatively calm market is the most conservative investment possible and consequently the safest. Unfortunately, bouts of frantic trading in the highly leveraged futures market can detract from the safety of gold and make the timing of a purchase crucial. With commodity futures you borrow virtually all the money for the purchase. It's risky, and it adds price volatility.

Another fly in the gold ointment could be the 1,118 million ounces of gold held by central banks. This represents approximately 1/3 of the above ground supply. Another 1/3 exists in gold jewelry and 1/3 is held by investors. Some central bank sold gold in the nineties. A desire for yields and more flexible reserves could spark a greater level of central bank selling. Nonchalance and an utter disregard for the role of gold among younger economists and bankers may also encourage selling over the longer term. Future central bank sales, however, will be tempered by a reluctance to damage the price of gold and hurt the value of their holdings along with the possibility of angering their citizenry and uncertainty about the future role of gold in monetary affairs.

With the exception of 1980, the one truly bad year in recorded history to buy gold, an investment in the yellow metal has essentially kept its value in terms of purchasing power. If you bought gold in 1974, two decades later in 1994, you still have a high value asset. Twenty years hence, you can be reasonably assured this value will still be there. You can't say that about anything else.

Gold represents the purest form of wealth, the elemental basis of riches, the absolute among assets. Because of its international recognition and demand, its liquidity surpasses that of any other asset. Whether in Tashkent or Timbuktu, a half-ounce of gold in your hand means the same thing to everyone.

Certain assets such as diamonds, rare stamps, or collectibles require expertise and may be affected by subjectivity or fads. Even real estate prices can be whipsawed by the skill of buyers or sellers, to say nothing about the effect of interest rates, taxes, or the economy. The value of the U.S. dollar can be eroded by inflation or by currency markets. Banks and bank accounts depend on interest rate fluctuations, the financial strength of banking institutions, governments, insurers, and guarantors. Stocks are inherently unstable, dependent on individual company performance, and the confidence of the crowd. None of these things affect gold. At any one time on this earth, a majority of the billions of inhabitants have, in the back of their mind, a hope, a wish, or a plan, to acquire more gold.

Gold futures, gold stocks, or gold options, don't fill the bill for most of the world's gold buyers. They want gold in their physical possession. These indirect methods of owning gold have their place but carry much greater levels of risk and monumental timing requirements. They are fluid while gold is solid. For example, in an extended stock market crash, gold stocks could decline while gold prices rise.

No person of means should be without some gold in his or her possession. In this country we have had the best of what the world has had to offer for as long as any of us can remember. This in itself is unusual. History offers too many pessimistic examples of the worst of all worlds. We prospered in America for a specific set of reasons. Now, a government at odds with the very reasons for our economic success has loaded the poor, old capitalist burro to the breaking point. Who knows what new weight will buckle the over-burdened beast.

Virtually every person can add up their net worth in a few seconds. A minimum of 5% of this figure should be held in physical gold. This pure form of wealth can backstop all other assets. It's your absolute, no-nonsense protection. It acknowledges that you think there is at least a one-in-20 chance that economic events will go seriously haywire. If you think the odds are even greater for a severe economic dislocation, then 10% in gold makes sense. Future events may require you to raise this percentage.

The present course of the U.S. government is leading to economic destruction. The dismal record of government-run economies leaves no room for optimism. The question is not if we will suffer an economic reckoning, the question is when! When that time comes, gold will be your best friend.

95

In this century most politicians have believed in a large, dominant role for government. Future centuries may think of the current period as the age of big government. This statism fosters socialism by installments. Some economists have described the mixed economy as a phase in the transition from capitalism to socialism.

We remain far from convinced that the public will part with its subsidies and government benefits. We suspect the American people want a certain level of socialism. This means frequent meddling in the market, a national ethic of handouts, and something for nothing, and unbridled government spending. These policies harm the economy. Socialist policies (call them liberal, democratic, populist or progressive) lower our living standards and erode the value of the dollar.

As long as this process continues, investors will have no choice but to look at gold as a way to offset losses to their dollar holdings. The dollar loses purchasing power when it declines against the Mark and the Yen. If you own gold, you can't get hurt by a devaluation. When the dollar declines, raw materials and products manufactured overseas cost more. Since we import more than a quarter of what we consume in the U.S., these products rise in price which causes price inflation at home.

People normally think that price inflation only accompanies an economic boom. That's because in the past consumer prices seemed to peak with the economy. Nowadays, price inflation clings stubbornly and hangs on even in a recession. As we said, much of this is caused by the fall of the dollar in foreign exchange markets.

The falling dollar may be the chief reason that gold would be good to own in a severe recession or depression. Foreigners would simply get out of dollars in a lack of faith gesture towards a failing economy. In this kind of environment when all assets plunge in value, gold would likely fall the least. Superimpose any kind of panic or fear on this situation, and the price of gold would explode upward.

The U.S. currency may be especially vulnerable in a depression or hyper-inflation because of the trillions of our dollars overseas. The dollar acts as the world's reserve currency much as gold once did. If the dollar continues to lose ground and dollar holders suffer losses, they may turn to another currency. A flight from the dollar could overwhelm the monetary authorities and sink the dollar. Certain foreign currencies (especially the German Mark) are strong enough to rival the dollar. A new European currency will soon compete with the dollar.

In the U.S. we consume more and produce less. Our chief economic rivals save and invest more. (This is so important that we say it a number of times in this book). Capital destruction, taxing, and spending, cause underinvestment rather than capital growth. Investments in shopping centers, commercial buildings and service industries take precedence over investments in manufacturing and production facilities.

Malinvestment makes recessions or depressions more likely. Poor economic performance means that more aggressive attempts at monetary easing (inflating) must be engineered by government to rescue the failing economy. Consequently, gold will likely play a role of growing importance. The worse the fate of the dollar, the more important the role of gold.

It's clear that the dollar is in trouble. In 50 years, over 90% of its purchasing power has disappeared. This trend remains intact and can worsen any time. Claims that gold will be less important in such an environment simply don't take into account the historical evidence. Whenever paper currencies have inflated away their value, the citizens of the countries involved have turned to gold.

As Ludwig von Mises pointed out, " In many parts of the earth an increasing number of people realize that the United States and most of the other nations are firmly committed to a policy of progressing inflation. They have learned enough from the experience of the recent decades to conclude that on account of these inflationary policies an ounce of gold will one day become more expensive in terms both of the currency of the United States and of their own country. They are alarmed and would like to avoid being victimized by this outcome."

Gold acts as a refuge from the effects of government blunders and mismanagement. The yellow metal protects against the ravages of socialism. As the economic damage mounts and a collapse looms closer, gold will be indispensable.

CHAPTER XVIII

HOW TO AVOID THE PITFALLS AND TRAPS IN GOLD INVESTMENTS

"With gold supply increasing at a slower pace and demand continuing its brisk rise, a small rise in investor interest in the yellow metal could produce a large run-up in its price. The investment sleeper of the 1990s, in sum, could be gold."

Barron's

"Every individual is a potential gold buyer, although he may not need the gold. It may be added to the store of personal wealth, and passed from generation to generation as an object of family wealth. There is no other economic good as marketable as gold."

Hans F. Sennholz

"To prefer paper to gold is to prefer high risk to lower risk, instability to stability, inflation to steady long term values, a system of very low grade performance to a system of higher, though not perfect, performance."

William Rees-Mogg

Much of the following information comes from the literature of the well known gold company, Investment Rarities Incorporated. We have reprinted a part of their information on the pitfalls of gold investing. This company provides educational material and economic newsletters that give excellent information on gold. They are also a good source for gold purchases. You can call them toll free at **1-800-328-1860** for literature on precious metals.

They issue this warning: "Although gold has gone up 1,000% in the past 25 years, some investors in the yellow metal have lost money. We want to show you the traps and pitfalls which triggered these losses and then tell you the exact way a few investors have made big profits in the gold market.

Gold or Silver Futures

By putting up a small amount of money, you can hold a futures contract on 100 ounces of gold. Generally you can make money if gold goes up sharply, right after you buy. However, the risks are too high for prudent investors.

If the price of the metal drops, you are required to come up with large sums for margin calls. Heavy trading activity in gold and silver usually means a whopping increase in the maintenance fee you must put up for each contract. This maintenance fee protects the brokerage firm if you fail to meet your margin call. There are also commissions and an interest charge built into the contract.

Some experts believe that 90% of all investors in commodity contracts suffer losses. Many professional speculators play this market, so you are competing against the best. Although commodity futures markets are the chief method of arriving at the daily price for gold and silver, they are generally too risky. Futures contracts are the direct opposite of a conservative gold investment strategy, wherein you take the actual gold into your possession.

Leverage Contracts

If you understand the risks in the futures market, you can clearly understand what's involved in one of the most heavily promoted methods of buying gold or silver - the leverage deal. Several private companies have flourished in the past two decades by offering these investments which are a disguised form of futures contracts.

In a leverage contract, the investor buys a specific amount of gold or silver. A large downpayment is required. Carrying costs and commissions are substantial. The metals are supposedly stored in a vault somewhere. In reality, the metals are only indirectly connected to your purchase through a futures contract, which backs up the deal.

In other words, many of the risks in a futures contract are present with a leveraged purchase. Companies who sell these contracts advertise heavily in major financial publications. Often these ads mention coins or bullion and imply that the metals are held in the investor's possession. However, leveraged positions are primarily trading vehicles and promote a short-term philosophy where the investor never sees the coins and bullion.

Furthermore, leverage contracts are more expensive than a futures contract and tend to be quite lucrative for the offering company. The investor would probably be much better off dealing directly in the futures market. Overall risk in leverage transactions seems too high for prudent investors who want to develop a winning long-term strategy.

Financed Purchases

A number of banks offer partial financing of precious metals and coin purchases. Interest costs and other charges or fees make financing gold a dubious proposition. The gains may not be high enough to absorb the costs and still leave a profit. Precious metals prices have a history of lying dormant for lengthy periods of time and then exploding upward in a short period. If your timing is perfect, you can come out O.K., but most such purchases have turned out to be money losers. Our strong recommendation is to avoid financing your gold purchase.

Gold and Silver Options

An option means that you have a right to the financial outcome of a futures contract. For an option fee, you can control a certain amount of gold or silver for several months.

Options limit the risk present in a futures contract. They can be profitable in a market moving in one direction. However, whenever the markets heat up, the fee or premium you pay to buy an option increases sharply. If the silver or gold prices don't go up enough to offset this stiff fee, you have lost that amount. However, that's all you can lose.

Commissions on options can be outrageous. For example, if you bought an option on silver for 60 days and the cost was $1,000, as much as $450 of that could be commission. Some firms charge less, but the commission is never low.

All the foregoing investments have one thing in common. The buyer never holds the gold in his or her possession. That's contrary to our bedrock advice. You cannot develop a prudent long-term investment strategy unless you get the coins and bullion into your possession.

Bullion Storage

This represents a different twist on taking the gold and silver under your control. You turn the physical purchase over to a storage facility and they charge you a fee to keep it there. Many of these storage facilities are first rate and hundreds of millions of dollars in precious metals sit in their subterranean vaults. Storage fees average 1/2 of 1% of total dollar value of coins or bullion.

Most companies who offer storage programs use storage facilities located in Delaware. These vaults seem safe, and the metals are insured. However, many storage agreements are between you and the company that sells the metals. They, in turn, have an agreement with the storage facility.

Never forget that gold and silver is a feast or famine business. Profits are low and dealer mortality high. You don't need to store your metal in the name of a company that has problems. If you decide to store your gold, get a storage agreement between you and the storage facility. When you sell, you must sign a release from the bank or vault before your metals are removed.

Credible storage facilities exist in Switzerland. Most large bullion dealers will have an arrangement through one of the principal bullion wholesalers to store at Mat Securitas Express AG/SA. Storage charges in Switzerland are 1/2% of gold or silver value. You can visit this facility at your convenience and view your gold.

While we favor taking gold into your possession, we realize there are times when this can be inconvenient. Also when you have much over a 1/2 million dollars of gold in your safe or deposit box, you need to find another alternative storage place for additional gold. Storage in a larger facility may be a sensible alternative for large amounts of the yellow metal.

Fraud

A number of major frauds in the past 20 years have centered around paper transactions and storage programs. To avoid problems, make the following concrete rules.

1. Never let any investment company hold or store your bullion or coins at their premises.

2. If you store your metals, try to make sure the storage plan is directly between you and the storage facility.

3. Never buy metals with a delayed delivery plan or where you are paid a fee to let the dealer use your metal.

4. Never make a down-payment and let the dealer hold your coins or bullion. Pay the full amount and take possession.

5. Never fall for purchase plans that offer coins or bullion under the spot price.

6. Never use a purchase plan that allows the dealer to hold the metal and pay you interest on the gold.

Most of the major scandals and frauds in the precious metal business could have been easily avoided if investors would have followed these simple rules. Too many investors jump at offers that are too good to be true. Always be leery of outrageous claims coming from brand new firms. A few years ago several scoundrels in Florida advertised they would sell gold at below the spot price. They would then hold the gold for six months before they sent it to you. How could anyone sell gold under the market price? Investors should have scorned them. Instead they sent them millions to get into this, too-good-to-be-true, offer. The crooks spent the money and never did have the gold. While they deserved to go to jail, the greedy and gullible investors had nobody to blame but themselves. Deal with reputable companies that have been in business for a number of years. If a company offers you something that seems too-good-to-be-true you can be sure that it is.

CHAPTER XIX

GOLD BULLION AND GOLD COINS

"Start now buying gold coins, any kind, and hoarding them."

Dr. John L. King

"The gold standard makes the money's purchasing power independent of the changing ambitions and doctrines of political parties and pressure groups. This is not a defect of the gold standard; it is its main excellence."

Ludwig von Mises

"Place 5 percent to 10 percent of your total assets in gold bullion and selected gold and silver coins. No one knows with certainty whether the coming depression will be inflationary or deflationary."

James Dale Davidson

Here are the ways that people own gold in their physical possession:

The U.S. Gold Eagle - This is the most popular gold bullion coin in America. These coins are struck by the U.S. Mint. The Eagle has exactly one ounce of gold with 1/2 ounce and smaller coins also available. The beautiful Walking Liberty on the Eagle duplicates the image of the famous Double Eagle that Teddy Roosevelt initiated in 1907.

The Austrian Philharmonics - This 24-Karat gold coin was introduced to gold investors in 1989 by the Austrian Mint, a subsidiary of Austria's Central Bank. The Philharmonic is minted in four sizes: one-ounce, half-ounce, quarter-ounce, and tenth-ounce. Comparable in price to the U.S. Eagle and the Canadian Maple Leaf, the Philharmonic's high face value - 2,000 Austrian Schillings or about U.S. $180 at recent exchange rates - is a popular feature with many investors. With sales of 590,000 ounces in 1992, the Vienna Philharmonic became the world's best-selling coin that year.

The Canadian Maple Leaf - This coin contains one pure ounce of gold. In the late 1970's the Krugerrand was the most popular gold coin in America. Then in 1986, when the importation of the Krugerrand was banned, the Maple Leaf became the leading gold bullion coin. Now it is second to the U.S. Eagle. However, investors become bored buying the same gold coin over and over again. They will diversify into the Maple Leaf and likely keep it popular in the U.S.

The Krugerrand - Up until the time they were banned, the South African Krugerrand was the most popular gold coin in the U.S. It's legal again to import Krugerrands. There already are millions of these coins in the U.S. An important component of the gold coin business is in the after-market. Most gold coins trade actively among dealers. The premiums can shrink on the major gold coins if the after-market supply exceeds demand. In the case of the Krugerrand, the premium has virtually disappeared. They trade close to their bullion value. They will never trade much below their bullion value and are still a worthwhile means to hold gold. The premium should resume now that they can be imported again.

Mexican 50 Pesos - This big coin weighs in at one and two-tenths of an ounce of gold. The Mexican government struck these coins with dies dated in the 40's so they are called restrikes. Back in the early 70's, before gold was legal, you could own them because the early dates made them legal. These coins have been around since the 70's, but have never caught on in a big way. When gold became legal in 1975, the South Africans rapidly outmarketed the competition and grabbed up a dominant share of the U.S. market.

Austrian and Hungarian 100 Coronas - These two coins are also both restrikes and contain 98/100 of one ounce of gold. They were extremely popular for a short time in the mid-70's and with any skilled marketing help could easily have become the number one coin in the U.S. However, as the Krugerrand took over, they faded. You can still buy them, but unless the price is quite favorable, we don't know why you would.

The Australian Kangaroo Nugget - The Kangaroo Nugget coin is a legal tender pure gold coin with pre-announced, limited annual mintages. The Kangaroo Nugget is competitively priced and is available in five sizes; 1 oz., 1/2 oz., 1/4 oz., 1/10 oz., and 1/20 oz.

Foreign Coins - Small foreign gold coins such as the French Rooster, Dutch Guilder, and Swiss Franc, are common bullion coins. There's nothing wrong with them, They are a good diversification. The biggest problem with these small coins has been price gouging. Certain dealers have sold these coins as rarities and marked them up double or triple over their true value.

Gold "Rounds" - Certain large refineries have minted one ounce gold "rounds" that supposedly compete with bullion coins. However, coin sized rounds such as the Prospector have never captured much of a following and remain a minor segment of the gold market.

Gold Bullion Bars - Gold bars have never been popular with U.S. investors. Gold coins outsell bars 100 to 1 among the American public. However, for large purchases that go into storage, gold bars may be suitable.

OTHER NEWLY MINTED GOLD COINS

Coins cover a wide spectrum, a few of which are questionable investments. We should cover the least appealing first.

Chinese Panda - These coins have been minted and promoted during the 80's. They are generally issued at a significant price premium over their melt down bullion value. Pandas became phenomenally popular among many dealers because of the markups and wider spreads. Consequently, they were heavily promoted, and the prices soared as much as 500% over the original issue price. Most

Pandas are one ounce gold coins with mintages as low as 15,000 coins in a given year.

We don't advocate ownership of newly minted foreign coins. However, in the marketplace, Pandas have proven to be popular. They have considerable beauty and it's hard to argue with their success. If you can buy these coins at prices reasonably close to bullion, then it doesn't hurt to own them.

Singapore Tigers - These coins fall into the category of too much of a good thing. The success of the Panda has drawn imitators. These are limited mintage gold coins designed to be instant rarities. The market could ultimately become saturated with new coin promotions and prices could drop to Krugerrand levels. All these coins mean overkill and in the past these newly minted fads have failed to hold up. Buy these at bullion coin prices rather than pay a big premium.

Newly Minted Foreign Coins - Special gold commemoratives from small countries, foreign Olympic coins, Pound, and Sovereign coins all have two things in common: they are pretty and they sell at a wide premium over their gold value. Investors should generally stay away from any collector coins minted in the past ten years. Give these coins a decade or two to season before you consider them.

Another wrinkle aimed at collectors is newly minted sets of medallions put out by private mints. They have no country sponsoring them and are not coin of the realm. Usually they commemorate certain people, characters or events. They sell at a significant premium over their melt value and should only be purchased for their beauty or collectability rather than as a hedge.

CHAPTER XX

THE BEST GOLD COLLECTOR COINS

"The standard of living of the common man is higher in those countries which have the greatest number of wealthy entrepreneurs."

Ludwig von Mises

"...there seems to be a correlation between the intensity of the official attacks on gold and the severity of monetary crises."

Hans F. Sennholz

"I see a great future for gold and silver coins as the currency people may increasingly turn to when paper currencies begin to disintegrate."

Murray M Rothbard

In this day and age, people collect virtually anything that's old. Baseball cards, old toys, antiques, stamps, duck decoys, furniture, pocket watches; you name it, somebody collects it. The highest quality items in these collectible categories bring a small fortune.

The desire to collect something old and historical also applies to coins. However, coins have something going for them to which no other collectible can lay claim. Coins have intrinsic value. You could melt them for the bullion value. Naturally, no one would ever do that. The gold content merely adds to their value and gives these coins the most unique of attributes. They can appreciate not only from collector demand, but also from a rise in gold prices. This two-sided value play makes old gold coins the most advantageous of collectible investments. They are superior, in many people's opinion, to bullion coins and are preferable to collectibles that have no intrinsic value.

Many gold buyers worry about the possibility of government confiscation of their gold. They prefer collector coins that have a small premium over their gold value but can be classified as historical or antique collector coins. The U.S. $20 gold pieces fill this particular niche better than any other.

When the U.S. confiscated gold in the 1930's they let citizens keep collector gold coins. When Lenin and Stalin purged and killed and seized assets, they let people keep gold collector coins. On the other hand, in the great gold purge of 1928-1929, they shot people for owning gold bullion.

You can buy a roll of 20 Double Eagles with at least ten different dates. That gives you a gold coin collection with a variety of mint marks and various dates. The strategy of buying collector coins has worked in past confiscation, and it should work in the off chance that such a thing would happen again, but it's no absolute guarantee.

Gold owners like privacy. They don't want the government to know that they own gold. A report to the government is not required at the time you buy gold. However, when you sell coins such as Krugerrands and Canadian Maple Leafs, the dealer must report your sale to the Treasury. Double Eagles, U.S. Eagles, and Austrian Philharmonics, are currently exempt from such reports. The trend in the future will probably be towards more reporting, and because the Double Eagles are not just bullion coins but also collector coins, they have a better chance of staying exempt.

CIRCULATED OR UNCIRCULATED?

The lowest priced antique U.S. gold coins are circulated. That means that they have some minor wear from passing through various hands after they were placed in circulation. Collectors prefer coins that are uncirculated and pay the highest price for coins that are free of marks, scratches, or blemishes. A rare high grade gold coin recently sold for $800,000.

When coins left the mint, they were placed together in bags and almost all such coins have "bag marks", which are small nicks and scrapes. Coins with the least marks bring the best prices.

Circulated U.S. gold coins are a low priced way to own 50 to 100 year old coins and a preferable alternative to the newly minted items of today. Antique U.S. gold coins in either circulated or uncirculated condition are one of the best options for gold coin buyers.

GRADING

U.S. coins in uncirculated condition are evaluated by a grading system which numbers the coins from Mint State 60 (MS-60) to Mint State 70 (MS-70); the latter being the highest grade a coin can attain. However, MS-70 coins are essentially perfect, and few, if any, such coins exist. Most high grade coins have some minor scratches that may only be visible under magnification. In fact, the perfect coin may not exist.

Coin grading services such as the Professional Coin Grading Service eliminate most of the grading risk from buying high priced and high grade rare gold coins. With lower grades or with circulated coins, this third party grading is not as necessary and may be too expensive.

MS-64 coins are easier to find, and so their price is less than a MS-65 coin. They are extremely attractive coins. MS-63 coins have a few more bag marks but still are attractive and have considerable demand. MS-61 and MS-62 have become popular coins. MS-60 coins are the lowest grade of the uncirculated coins but are more attractively priced. Their bullion content is a big factor in their value. They are excellent coins and should be included in most gold coin portfolios.

Circulated gold coins are graded from the well-worn to those that are almost uncirculated. Investors should concentrate on the VF grade (very fine), up to the XF grade (extremely fine), and then to the AU grade (almost uncirculated). These are the highest grades of circulated coins.

19TH AND EARLY 20TH CENTURY U.S. GOLD COINS

Without question, the most popular U.S. gold coins are the Double Eagles. These are $20 gold pieces that contain just under one ounce of gold (.9675).

Liberty Head - This Double Eagle was minted from 1849 to 1907. We recommend this 100 year old coin for purchase in both circulated and uncirculated. Libertys become more difficult to find in MS-63 and MS-64 grades and prices reflect this scarcity. The less expensive XF coins and MS-60 grade coins represent the best gold value for the money.

Saint-Gaudens - Many coin experts claim the Saint-Gaudens to be the most beautiful coin ever minted. The new U.S. Eagle bullion coin copied the design of the Saint-Gaudens. These coins were minted off and on from 1907 to 1933. However, none of the latter year was placed in circulation. The lowest priced Saints are several of the more common dates, while the rare 1927D sells for up to $800,000. The Saint-Gaudens is perhaps the premier U.S. coin, and investors should consider it in all grades.

$10 Liberty Head - This mainstay of 19th century U.S. coinage was minted from 1866 to 1907. An earlier and more expensive Coronet style was minted from 1838 to 1866. These coins contain just under one-half ounce of gold. They can be a sound investment in all grades.

$10 Indian Head Type - This beautiful coin shows Liberty crowned with an Indian war bonnet. These coins are more expensive than the $10 Liberty. Although minted from 1907 to 1933, mintages were small.

Minor U.S. Gold Coins - The Liberty Head coins were minted as $5.00 Half Eagles and $2.50 Quarter Eagles. The $2.50 coins were minted in small numbers and are scarce in uncirculated condition. The more common $5.00 coins carry a lower premium over their gold bullion value and are a good investment choice. Sets of the four denominations of Liberty have considerable popularity.

In 1908, and for a number of years thereafter, $5.00 and $2.50 Indian Head coins were minted at the various U.S. mints. These unusual coins were struck with an incuse design where the Indian and Eagle are sunk into the coin's surface. Investors should secure these coins individually or in sets.

Minor U.S. Gold Rarities - The U.S. also struck $1.00 gold coin and $3.00 gold pieces. These coins minted in the mid to late 19th century are found in limited numbers. They sell for high prices that have no relationship to their gold content.

Numismatic Gold - For the advanced collector, a number of numismatic treasures exist. Eagles and Half Eagles were minted as early as 1795. A $4 gold coin, the Stella, is one of the most valuable coins in our history.

Special rarities, like the 1907 Saint-Gaudens struck in high relief, command big prices. Gold commemorative coinage from the early 1900's is highly prized, and the two oversized varieties of the $50 Panama-Pacific coin are worth a small fortune. Numerous gold coins struck in the early West by a variety of private pioneer mints are another highly valuable segment of U.S. gold coin collecting.

THE COIN SWITCH THAT CAN HURT YOU.

A number of coin dealers tout rare coins as a superior investment to gold. That's a mistake. Many dealers try to switch people out of their gold Krugerrands and Double Eagles into high grade rare coins. This policy will work to everyone's disadvantage in the long run. Rare coins are not a proxy for gold ownership. They will not perform exactly as does gold, nor will they protect you in a depression. They should only be purchased after a basic position of gold ownership has been established. Don't trade gold coins for rarities. Add rare coins only if you enjoy collecting and only after you have at least 10% of your assets in gold.

CHAPTER XXI

KEEPING WHAT YOU HAVE

"Nothing beats a little cash in a bear market, of course, and the oldest form of cash is gold.

James Grant

"Gold is as steady as a rock, a standardbearer by which all currencies can be accurately measured."

Mark Skousen

"Buy gold and sit on it. That is the key to success."

Dr. Franz Pick

The average investor thinks more about making money than about keeping it. People focus on gains or income but pay little attention to the threat of losing in a major way. Virtually no one prepares against the risk of great loss. They belittle the idea of a crash or panic that bankrupts the institutions and wipes them out personally. We have been rolling along for so long without a major financial disaster that most people no longer consider such an event possible.

If you have ever started a business and tried to make a profit, you know how tough it is to make money. It can take years of work and struggle to get into the black. Conversely, it's been quite easy to make money investing in stocks. Lately it's been easier than ever to harvest these gains. In the past you needed patience coupled with sound investment principals to make money in stocks. Now stock gains come quickly and virtually every investor seems to profit.

Despite a few mild recessions, the years since the end of the second war have been the Golden Age of investment. Recently it's been a period of worry-free financial affairs. Prior to the past fifty-years the U.S. was racked by depressions, panics and hyper-inflations. In fact, throughout history, there have been regular intervals when credit collapses, panics, hyper-inflations and depressions ruined countries and currencies and turned the rich into poor. In other words, the past five decades of investment bliss are the exception rather than the rule.

Nobody worries about a big crash or panic. They've never experienced such an animal. The widespread belief that the government won't let anything bad happen reinforces the view that they are immune to destructive losses. Consequently, almost no one takes any measure at all to protect themselves against the financial plagues that have regularly afflicted mankind.

Not only are many individuals totally invested in stocks and mutual funds, they have their entire retirement plan committed to equities. Some add leverage to the mix and borrow additional money for stocks. Others run down cash balances and savings to buy stocks. A dip in stock prices fosters additional buying rather than any serious concern about further declines. Virtually all of today's investors are on the offensive. No one plays defense.

People apply the least shrewd thinking to their retirement money. Here's the mindset: Our retirement plan is a long-term investment and we will leave it in stocks through rain or shine and it will always trend higher in the long run. Eventually any loss will be made up. That thinking may make more sense at the end of a bear market but not when the bull has broken all the records. People who have never been in a bear market or who believe the Wall Street propaganda about a permanent boom will be devastated by the bear. The bear brings financial disaster and a kind of fear that changes the way people behave and think for years to come.

Everyone in the market makes the assumption that they can get out before a big downward slide. In other words, they will be able to see trouble before other investors and thus make their exit. Past market reversals generally follow a pattern of steep repetitive drops wiping out as much as half the bull-market gains within a few weeks. The bear doesn't ring a warning bell. The way people have deluded themselves about a perpetual bull market means that many will decide to weather the decline. These folks will keep on believing that it will bounce back. They will hold till late in a decline and thereby sacrifice years of gains. In the worst bear market drops, it's entirely possible that you can't get out at anywhere near the quoted price. With enough sellers and a panic atmosphere, bids vanish and prices go through the floor. Sell orders get triggered at much lower prices. Mutual fund liquidations may be held up for days while markets plummet. At times, in severe shakeouts you can't get out at all. The idea that the stock market possesses unparalleled liquidity is a myth. Rather, it could become quite illiquid.

Sixty years ago the country struggled in a depression that lasted eight years. Severe stock market losses wiped out the wealth of investors and illustrated that it's entirely possible to lose everything in a market crash. Whenever such an event begins in earnest, fear turns into panic, losses jump quickly and values evaporate. Today's bear market virgins have never experienced such a crisis. They will turn into nasty, snarling lunatics, terrified by mounting losses should the bear strike. Some will go out the window.

John Pugsley warns, "A massive amount of institutional money is being invested by professional managers whose sum total of bear market experience consists of the sharp but temporary market correction of 1987. Felix Rohatyn, one of the industry's most respected stock market observers, put it concisely when he noted that Wall Street is now in the hands of a bunch of 26-year-old kids with computers who are creating a financial hydrogen bomb."

As it did in 1929, when it started a depression, another great stock crash can lead to a steep plunge in business activity. Confidence fades fast in a financial crisis. Consumer spending slows way down and savings rise. With the massive amount of credit card debt, consumer loans and extremes of leverage throughout the financial system a stiff recession can turn nasty. That's when people lose their jobs, can't pay their bills, have their cars repossessed and lose their homes.

How many people won't be able to pay their mortgages, bills, and credit cards if the market crashes or if the economy slows, or both? Has Wall Street set a trap for the wealth of America? In time, we will know the answers. In the interim, it appears to be a time when defensive measures make sense.

It's pure speculation on my part, but having watched carefully the market corrections of the past few years, it seemed that each time a downturn threatened to get out of hand, a powerful surge of buying would appear. Could this be a buying pool of banks or brokerage firms financed in some way by the monetary authorities? This would account for the unprecedented bull market because normal corrections were never allowed to run their course. I dismissed the idea as the machinations of a mind overly anxious for a gold boom. However, were it true, it would set the stage for an even greater market collapse.

Recently, however, I read Chairman Alan Greenspan's comments in a speech he gave in Belgium. "We have the responsibility to prevent major financial market disruptions through development and enforcement of prudent regulatory standards and, if necessary, in rare circumstances through direct intervention in market events." Say what? Regulators have the responsibility of direct intervention in markets? This certainly represents a dramatic broadening of the role of the Central Bank. We need more clarification on this point. However, if the aim is to support the dollar, bolster the stock market, hold up the bond market, keep the economy humming, and fight inflation, even the most powerful interventionists can bite off more than they can chew and wind up failing at all.

Even government securities can turn sour if the credit-worthiness of government comes into question. Throughout history those governments that spent wantonly and borrowed recklessly usually defaulted. The citizens of these countries never got advance notice. They were wiped out. In our modern era when gold has no role as money and nothing can put a brake on monetary expansion the Central Bank can monetize any amount of debt. So rather than default, the government can inflate the debt away. In either case the bondholder gets killed.

People have the mistaken belief that good times can't change. Few have the historical perspective to understand just how much suffering past economic failures have caused. They don't appreciate how good this country has had it or what a remarkably luxurious life they have. Most people who lived in prior times suffered in conditions we would consider harsh and cruel. The periodic loss of what little they had was the nature of things.

Just as we have rolled back disease we have rolled back financial perils. But just as we can still be killed by illness, our economy and financial markets can be destroyed by unsound practices. We've had it too good for too long. Nature has never allowed a nation to experience unbroken prosperity nor has it ever allowed a people to indulge themselves and become spoiled for long. Nature presents us with regular doses of hardship, disappointment, struggle, pain and poverty. We've broken too many rules to avoid this retribution. Our finances are so far off track that the scope of our ultimate financial collapse can't be comprehended.

Most market commentary expresses little or no concern about such a steep correction. Wall Street preaches permanent boom, endless prosperity, and a perpetual bull market. Downturns are only opportunities. Even a nasty decline of 10 percent to 20 percent is viewed as a healthy purging of excesses before another big upturn begins.

When you have high levels of money and credit creation funneling into stocks, along with rampant leverage, record margin debt, inflated stock values, and swollen historical ratios, you have far greater potential for a monumental bust. We're not talking about a simple correction, we're talking about a debt collapse, deflation and depression. Blood does not run in the streets after a period of prudent investment and modest speculation. But it does occur following excesses similar to those present in today's market. Nevertheless, the public remains impervious to just how lethal things can get. History shows us that booms turn to busts. The term bear market defines what used to be a frequent market phenomenon that's erased from the minds of today's investors. From every historical perspective a big, mean bear market is long overdue. Whether we can withstand such a market without an economic and credit collapse is the $64,000 question.

The worst feeling in the world comes when liquidity vanishes. When you must sell and you can't, then fear and anxiety replace the self-assurance and certainty of better days. Shrinking liquidity often escalates into panic. Liquidity can disappear in any market and requires major downward price adjustments. Prices simply evaporate and losses become unbearable. Panic selling overwhelms the market.

With huge losses in world markets enough red flags are in the wind to go on the defensive. The extent of the destruction of wealth in Asia defies comprehension. What you can gain today in stocks compared to what you can lose, doesn't match up. Small investors hold the market up by diving in on any decline. These investors have generally always been wrong. It's been rewarding to be opposite them.

Richard Russell of The Dow Theory Letter talks about the bear luring in as many investors as possible before he strikes. The bear is out to destroy as much money as he can and he disguises his actions to fool people into thinking he is weak. He strikes when investors are most credulous and unsuspecting.

A market crash can dramatically slow the economy. Loans go into default, bankruptcies soar, stocks plummet and losses mount. Business slows and layoffs escalate. Scandals erupt as the imprudent and dishonest see their schemes unravel in the glare of a merciless market. The lenders who have had their day in the sun take hit after hit. Wealth shrinks and prices of all assets erode. In the face of a great rush for liquidity, liquidity wanes.

The small guy grits his teeth and weeps each morning as he reads the stock quotes. His relatives second guess him to distraction. He constantly seeks reassurance from brokerage firm spokesmen on TV. Worry becomes a constant companion. Decisions become irrational. He digs in and refuses to sell anything. His broker owns the same stocks and he agrees.

Large leverage players and international money management stars take a pounding. Big money interests pull in their horns. Assets under management shrivel and sophisticated money goes to the sidelines. Activity diminishes. Volume drops. The game is over. Legions of burned investors sue.

Unemployment mounts. Tax receipts fall and budget deficits grow. The government must return tax money for losses on stock transactions. Unemployment benefits and social costs demand greater government spending. GNP shrinks and corporate profits erode. Massive layoffs cause civil disturbances and unrest. Leftists become media darlings. Government mortgage and loan guarantees require billions as failures and bankruptcies reach epidemic proportions. Runaway U.S. budget deficits require massive funding. Special interest rate deals appear. Municipalities go broke.

The dollar takes a vicious drop. The Fed strives to push interest rates lower and sinks the dollar further. Foreigners, gripped by a sickening downward spiral of domestic asset values, sell whatever is liquid and U.S. bonds go out the window. U.S. interest rates see-saw as dollar dumping gains impetus. Politicians and monetary officials make frequent reassurances and daily promises that are broken on the following day.

A wave of bankruptcies sweep financial service companies. Brokerages and management companies implode. Home values drop by a third or more. Loan and mortgage companies succumb. Credit card companies beg the government for a bailout. Small banks fail and big banks get round after round of government transfusions.

Conditions worsen. The unthinkable happens. The U.S. government fails to fund certain programs and delays some major payments. Government guarantees on loans gone sour stack up unpaid. Decades of credit expansion disintegrate into a monumental debt collapse that threatens the solvency of the government. The economy is ruined.

Make no mistake about it, a debt-driven consumption boom in conjunction with a credit-driven speculative boom can explode like a double-barreled shotgun next to your ear. Will it happen? Who knows? The point is that it can happen. It's no way a remote possibility. Something like it happened in Asia and the U.S. commits most of the same economic sins.

Virtually everyone holds their financial assets within a system that depends on outside circumstances for value. High stock prices depend on a continuing stream of new money and good business performance. Bonds depend on sound corporate finances. Treasury Bills and bonds depend on government solvency. Bank accounts depend on credit creation and government guarantees. Most of our nation's wealth lies within a government nurtured system. Deposits are guaranteed and only mainstream investments are encouraged by the financial and political establishment. That's how they make their money. But all these assets depend on something else for their value. They don't stand alone. For the most part they are inter-twined, all dependent on one another and back-stopped by government insurance and guarantees on a monumental scale.

Commercial real estate falls within this investment mainstream and home ownership has immense government financial support. But real estate values depend upon the effectiveness of government and central bank manipulation of the economy and in many cases government guarantees and supports. Real estate forms another part of the financial system that depends on outside factors for a good share of its value.

Collectibles such as antiques and art don't depend on government or business solvency for value. However, they do depend on the general health of the economy. A depression can easily cause these items to plunge along with all other assets.

The one asset least affected by economic performance, business solvency, government guarantees, or insurance is gold. The yellow metal depends on no institution or government for value. Gold exists outside the mainstream and depends on none of the same things that stocks, bonds and banks depend on. Gold means independence. Gold allows the citizen to escape total reliance on the state-sponsored financial system. It's a perfect asset for ultimate protection, no matter how dicey things get. Gold's value may be affected by the U.S.'s economic performance, but far less than other assets. In fact, if the mainstream financial system breaks down gold goes up because people turn to gold in a crisis. Gold does best when everything else suffers.

Most people have their assets within the Wall Street - Washington financial axis. Many are totally dependent for retirement benefits and income from this alliance of government, business and central bank. It's where everybody keeps their money.

That's because the people believe the government will always protect and take care of them. Of course the government wants to foster economic growth, prosperity, security and investment profits. But the government also takes strong measures to improve education, eliminate crime, improve race relations and eliminate poverty, to mention but a few of it's notorious failures. In other words, the government's gross ineptitude and rank political motivations make the outcome of their insurance, influence and intervention in the markets unworthy of anyone's total trust and reliance for their financial security.

CHAPTER XXII

GOLD CONFISCATION

"Whenever an overall breakdown of a monetary or financial system occurs, return to gold always restores order, revives confidence and brings back prosperity."

Donald Hoppe

"The possibility of a discriminatory capital-gains tax on gold 'profits,' or even of outright confiscation, cannot be wholly dismissed. We must remember that in 1933, when private citizens began to exercise their clear legal right to convert their Federal Reserve notes and gold certificates into gold, President Franklin D. Roosevelt suspended the conversion, ordered the citizens to exchange their gold for paper money, and made it illegal for private citizens to hold or own gold. In other words, the government not only broke its solemn and explicit pledge to convert its notes into gold on demand, but treated the holder (and dupe) who had taken the pledge seriously as the real culprit."

Henry Hazlitt

"The authorities in the United States confiscated private gold holdings in the Depression of the 1930's. They may seek to do so again in the Depression of the 1990's."

*James Dale Davidson and
Lord William Rees-Mogg*

This chapter is a condensation of David Schectman's, "White Paper on Gold".

When Franklin Roosevelt was inaugurated on March 4, 1933, economic conditions were so bad that a situation comparable to panic existed. More than twelve million people were out of work, and unemployment stood at 24.9 percent. Bread and soup lines stretched endlessly through city streets to feed the thousands who had absolutely nothing.

Four thousand banks failed that year. Three-fourths of them were Federal Reserve Banks. Nearly 32,000 businesses failed the year before, and total national production had dropped nearly 50 percent since 1929. Ninety percent of the values of the stock market were wiped out in the preceding two and a half years, and the Dow stood at 41.22. Mass withdrawals of bank deposits and "hoarding" of gold by individuals had reached a point that threatened destruction of the banking system.

Roosevelt took decisive action. His first official act on March 6, was a staggering proclamation that reverberated a mixture of hope and fear. He ordered every bank in the nation closed and prohibited paying out gold or dealing in foreign exchange. Three days later, he summoned a special session of Congress to confirm his actions and passed the Emergency Banking Act. The questionable authority of the old 1917, "Trading With the Enemy Act", was invoked to justify the action under the premise of a national emergency.

The new act empowered the President and the Treasury to maintain complete control over all transactions in gold, silver, and foreign exchange. The bank holiday was extended for another week to allow time for inspection and in-house audits by Federal Reserve examiners.

On April 5, 1933, another executive order was issued demanding COMPLETE SURRENDER OF GOLD COINS, GOLD BULLION, AND GOLD CERTIFICATES still in possession of individuals. The order directed that they be turned in to the nearest Federal Reserve Bank within 25 days. FAILURE TO COMPLY WAS PUNISHABLE BY A FINE OF $10,000 OR TEN YEARS IN PRISON OR BOTH.

This ended the 141-year era of circulating gold coins as a strong part of our monetary system. During the remainder of 1933, the President and the Treasurer issued additional regulations and clarifications on gold surrender. One exemption was authorized which permitted the holding of gold under special license for use in industry, certain professions, and RARE AND UNUSUAL COINS OF VALUE TO COLLECTORS.

The price of gold had been arbitrarily set at $20.67 a fine ounce for 96 years. The difference between the nominal value of the gold dollar and the actual gold content by weight was due to the original seigniorage granted the Treasury by law in 1837. Under this decree, a troy ounce of bullion worth $20.67 was exchanged for $20.00 in coin. The difference was allowed to offset minting costs.

Citizens who surrendered their gold were paid $20.67 per ounce in Federal Reserve Notes and silver coins. At the time of the surrender, the government gold stockpile stood at about 200 million ounces, or $4 billion at $20.67 per fine ounce.

ROOSEVELT DEVALUED THE DOLLAR BY 59%

In June, 1933, Congress passed a joint resolution abrogating gold clauses in all contracts past and future. This meant that all contractual obligations must be met in units of current currency value. Just six months later, on January 15, 1934, the Gold Reserve Act was passed authorizing all monetary gold to be owned by the government as a bullion base for its currency. All gold in the Federal Reserve was transferred to the Treasury in exchange for non-circulating gold certificates issued to Federal Reserve Banks. This Gold Reserve Act kicked off a series of events that shocked conscientious monetary thinkers and changed the face of the "New Deal" from wonder to suspicion.

The new law gave Roosevelt power to devalue the dollar in an amount he deemed appropriate, but not to exceed 60 percent. He jumped on it immediately and devalued the dollar 41 percent — from $20.67 per fine ounce of gold to $35. At the same time, he formally prohibited the minting of all gold coins and demonetized those outstanding. The devaluation netted the government a $3 billion profit and raised the value of its gold holdings to $7 billion. From the moment of the devaluation, the United States began to accumulate gold on an ever increasing scale. By 1940 our gold reserve had increased to $18 billion.

NEXT CAME THE CONFISCATION OF SILVER. On August 9, 1934, a Presidential Proclamation ordered all silver bullion surrendered to the Treasury within 90 days and a 50 percent TAX WAS LEVIED ON ANY PROFITS from the sale of silver. The order netted 113 million ounces for which the holders were paid 50.1 cents per ounce.

Most people don't realize that THE GOVERNMENT STILL HAS THE POWER TO SEIZE THIS GOLD. According to Ron Paul, a former Representative from the State of Texas:

"When the freedom to own gold was restored in 1975, a little known provision of the Federal Reserve Act was overlooked: 12 U.S.C. 248(n). This subsection outlines an authority, which, in effect, would negate the freedom granted in 1975 that allowed U.S. citizens to once again own gold. The law states:

"Whenever, in the judgment of the Secretary of the Treasury, such action is necessary to protect the currency system of the United States, the Secretary—at his discretion, may require any or all individuals— to pay and deliver to the Treasurer of the United States any or all gold coins, gold bullion, and gold certificates owned by such individuals.'

"In other words, we have on the books the power of the Government to abrogate the freedom of individuals to hold a specific commodity, in this case gold."

In a recent interview, Mr. Paul said:

"I served on the Gold Commission for eight or nine months while I was in Congress along with fifteen other members.

I brought up the subject of confiscation. The power to confiscate gold is still on the books as the law of the land. I urged the full Commission to recommend that Congress repeal the power to confiscate gold in an economic emergency.

"We pushed it to a vote and I was the only one that voted to recommend to Congress that we never again contemplate taking the gold of the American people. The 15 other members voted it down. The power is still there, on the books, and they can do it any time they wish."

Incidentally, in America we have had four different gold confiscations. The first two were during runaway inflations in Colonial America and the Revolutionary War. Next during the Civil War (in the south) and, of course, most currently during the banking crisis of 1933.

Gold confiscation always happens quickly, and without notice. You have a matter of days or weeks to turn over your gold. That law, however, does leave a loophole for legal ownership. Exempted from the surrender requirement were not the "owners" of rare gold coins, or "holders" of them, nor persons who "possessed" such coins, nor even "investors". On the contrary, the order specifically focused on an individual's motives for having rare gold coins, exempting just one classification: "collectors". There is a clear distinction between "collectors" and "investors" in rare coins.

A collector's primary interest in rare coins is enjoyment. It's for historical, aesthetic or cultural reasons. An investor's interest in rare coins is financial—to make a profit. Roosevelt clearly intended to exclude only the collector.

Subsequent Treasury legislation added to the original Executive Order the amendment stating, "Gold coin made prior to 1934 is considered to be of recognized special value to collectors of rare and unusual coins."

Economic historian, Franz Pick, had this to say about gold confiscation:

"I am afraid that one day the government will indeed call gold in. Gold bullion will be subject to confiscation.

"This is one big advantage to numismatic gold, such as the Double Eagles. It is an idiosyncrasy of governments that although they may prohibit ownership of gold in any form, they are reluctant to touch collections of numismatic gold coins.

"Today, there are some 49 countries which forbid ownership of gold by their citizens, but they do allow holding gold coins for numismatic purposes. Even the Soviet Union and Eastern European countries legally tolerate the acquisition of numismatic gold coins. So these are the only gold holdings that could be kept in your safe deposit box without any fear of confiscation."

WOULD THIS HOLD UP IN THE FUTURE IN CASE OF ANOTHER EMERGENCY CONFISCATION?

The answer is probably yes. The Eminent Domain clause of the Fifth Amendment of the U.S. Constitution stands between the rare coin collector and government confiscation. Part of the Eminent Domain clause states "....nor shall private property be taken (by the government) for public use, without just compensation."

Bullion was easy to confiscate at the official price in 1933. Payment was made at the "official" gold price of $20.67/ounce. What would have been a "fair price" for rare gold coins? This would have created tremendous difficulties. Coins would have to be judged on a per-coin basis which was simply impractical.

Editors Note:

In 1933 gold was confiscated to prop up the dollar and provide international solvency for the U.S. Today the gold held by U.S. citizens would not be near enough to accomplish that task. U.S. citizens probably own much less gold today per capita than in the 1930's when gold certificates were a claim on gold.

In other words, gold would not be confiscated for the same reason today. Furthermore, the U.S. mint sells gold coins that it mints for public purchase. It would take extraordinary circumstances to stop gold sales to citizens and take the gold back from them they have already purchased.

A more likely scenario would be the discontinuation of gold sales in the U.S. altogether. A ban on new sales could result from a domestic run from the dollar into gold. In other words, if gold began to compete with the dollar, the government would stop all gold sales. That possibility seems far more likely than an outright seizure and confiscation.

However, should enough gold pour into the country from private purchases, and should this buying go on for a period of time so that massive private reserves were built up, then the equation would be changed. At that juncture, politicians and bureaucrats may have little compunction over seizing gold. In fact, they would probably couple this action with public censure of gold holders. Greedy speculators and gold hoarders would make handy scapegoats for those looking to blame the coming monetary mess on someone other than themselves.

132

CHAPTER XXIII

GOLD - WHERE DOES IT COME FROM AND WHERE DOES IT GO!

"From a strictly economic point of view, buying gold in a major inflation and holding it probably presents the least risk of capital loss of any investment or speculation."

Henry Hazlitt

"An ounce of gold is an ounce of gold, whether it consists of guineas, sovereigns or eagles."

Hans F. Sennholz

"Regardless of the dollar price involved, one ounce of gold would purchase a good-quality man's suit at the conclusion of the Revolutionary War, the Civil War, the presidency of Franklin Roosevelt, and today."

Peter A. Burshre

Gold is found everywhere in microscopic amounts. The secret is to find a way to extract or mine it profitably.

The majority of the gold mined in the world has come from South Africa. South African mines extend deep in the ground and are costly to operate. Although the South African mines are slowly losing production, they still account for over 40% of the world's annual gold mining supply. A few years ago they amounted to 60%, so the present trend means less gold from South Africa.

In the 1980's the United States offset South Africa's production decline. The U.S. and Canada account for 25% of world production. U.S. gold production is centered in Nevada (60% of the U.S. total).

About 20% of the world's production comes from Russia. No one knows for sure the extent of Russia's gold mining since they have been secretive with production data. The disintegration of socialism will likely reduce Russian gold production for a while. Until the necessary capital rebuilds their gold industry, the Russians could be marginal producers. In the years ahead, big increases in gold production are expected from Mexico, South America, and Asia.

About 90% of the 120,000 metric tons of gold that have ever been mined still exist in the form of bars, coins and jewelry. This may make some gold investors nervous. However, since fully a third of this supply is in jewelry it won't hit the market in quantity. The market only uses about 3,000 tons of gold each year. That means a large above ground supply will always overhang the market. Furthermore, government and private holders are unlikely sellers of massive amounts of gold.

Between 10% and 15% of each year's gold supply comes from scrap. This includes melting old coins and jewelry. Around 90% of the annual supply comes from mining. Of the gold available annually from all sources, three quarters goes into the fabrication of gold jewelry and coinage. Italy remains the world's largest fabricator of gold jewelry, followed by the U.S., India, and Japan. Demand for jewelry continues to grow at a phenomenal rate, and for the long term, the annual supply of gold will likely be fully utilized. The balance goes to private hoarders and industrial users (about 6% of this for electronics). Author Timothy Green discusses this industrial use, "The realization that gold was not just a precious and beautiful metal, but also a versatile and useful one, goes back to the earliest civilizations. Modern technology, however, has found that its traditional virtues of malleability, ductility, reflectivity, and resistance to corrosion, are matched with unparalleled ability as a thermal and electrical conductor. Moreover, once you ally its resistance to corrosion with the facility to convey a tiny electrical current in temperatures varying from -55 to +200 degrees C, then you have one of the foundation stones of modern electronics. I always remember a scientist at Johnson Matthey, the precious metals specialists, saying many years ago, 'When people want something to be 500 percent reliable for twenty years, we recommend gold.' But, mindful of advances in technology, I recently asked an American electronics expert what substitute might be in view. 'Gold is still better than anything else we have evaluated,' he replied. In short, the phrase 'nothing is as good as gold', often used to advertise jewelry, ought really to be the motto for its industrial and decorative uses. Indeed, bypassing for a moment gold's more traditional applications in decoration and dentistry, one must acknowledge that our present age of high technology finds it indispensable in everything from pocket calculators to computers, telephones to television, and missiles to spacecraft."

Higher prices for gold in the 1970's and 1980's unleashed a mining boom and production increases. That growth has slowed down. However, some experts predict a resumption of this trend. With demand rising, higher prices will stimulate new mining sources and increase production.

In the late 1980's both Europeans and Americans have sold millions of ounces of gold. This has been more than offset by investors buying in other countries. Citizens of newly prosperous Asian countries with a history of political or military turmoil are the biggest buyers. In the 1980's, Japan ranked first among buyers, closely followed by Taiwan. They may now be overtaken by mainland China, which continues to be a growing gold buyer. The beneficial inroads of capitalism promise to dramatically increase the ability of the Chinese to purchase gold. Hong Kong and Singapore are also major buyers.

Long term trends indicate a strong demand for gold and a slowly shrinking level of production. This can be offset if high prices bring marginal mines into production. Monetary buying and a lively jewelry market promise to drive up prices. Gold jewelry sales are strong and even a worldwide recession didn't temper demand in Asia.

Timothy Green explains the great appeal of gold as jewelry, "The original appeal of gold as it gleamed warmly in the rivers and streams of Africa, Asia, and South America was its beauty. At the dawn of civilization, craftsmen found that it could be worked and fashioned with ease into magnificent ornaments and articles of adornment to enhance the human body. The basic techniques they perfected three and four thousand years ago, of drawing gold into wire to make into delicate filigree or foxtail chains, of casting it into a thousand shapes of flowers, birds and animals, that could also easily be engraved, have changed little. Nor has the basic fact that as we go towards the twenty-first century, gold jewelry remains the premier use of gold. Indeed, in 1992, the fabrication of carat gold jewelry worldwide exceeded the entire output of the mining industry for the first time Jewelry is the cornerstone of the gold business. The real difference though, is that what was virtually, until this century, the metal of the privileged and wealthy, is today within the means of millions. Gold Jewelry has become a mass market consumer item anywhere from Birmingham (England or Alabama) to Berlin, Bahrain, Bombay, Bangkok, and Beijing. Diamonds, so the catch-phrase goes, are forever; gold jewelry is for everyone, everywhere."

Proof that gold is the ultimate hedge against inflation and economic problems can be found in newly prosperous Brazil. This country has severe inflation and currency controls, so demand for gold has soared. Whenever a national currency appears to be shaky and there is some wealth, the citizens rapidly turn to gold.

The wild card in the gold equation is mainland China, where demand for gold exploded in 1992. Economic growth fosters this growing demand in an area of the world where gold is cherished. If every Chinese were to own one ounce of gold it would take all the world's gold mining production for years to come.

Gold stock broker, Blake Joyner, described a trip to Asia in 1993, "In Kuching, Sawarak, the Malaysian half of the island of Borneo, I was astonished by what I saw in the street bazaars. Forty or fifty percent of the women were wearing gold--many wore substantial amounts. This in a land that reported its last active head hunters seven years ago. What is responsible for this increased demand in Kuching? The same as elsewhere in Asia; rising wealth and a strong cultural affinity for gold.

"In Hong Kong, it is impossible to miss the enormous emphasis that Chinese place on gold. Jewelry shops on every block, have turbaned Sikhs with shotguns standing guard. Dragons, fish and other animals made of 24 carat gold are everywhere costing $15,000 - $30,000, but selling for only 15% above the melt value of the gold. It was difficult to find a Hong Kong woman not wearing gold.

"Even more surprising was my first visit to Canton in 19 years. The rice paddies and vegetable gardens of my memories of 20 years ago, were now apartment buildings and factories. Instead of the ugly Mao jackets of years ago' many young women now wore mini-skirts and small pieces of cheap gold jewelry. It is estimated that one Cantonese in five bought gold last year. That's one million buyers of gold in one Chinese city! Five million Chinese bought gold in 1993. With a GNP growing at 10% - 15% this year, a savings rate of 38% (the world's highest), and an ancient obsession with gold, tens of millions of Chinese will become new gold owners."

Recent changes in Asian wealth have cut into jewelry demand but gold still has a big following in the East. That's not likely to change much in our lifetime.

CHAPTER XXIV

GOLD STOCKS - FOLLOW THE CANADIANS

"When you buy gold equities you're buying gold that hasn't yet been mined. Making an astute investment will demand an understanding not only of the forces that drive gold prices but also a grasp of the workings of the stock market and the fundamentals of the stock - the company's reserves, production costs, earnings, dividends and management."

Pierre Lassonde

"The great merit of gold is precisely that it is scarce; that its quantity is limited by nature; that it is costly to discover, to mine, and to process; and that it cannot be created by political fiat or caprice."

Henry Hazlitt

"As the prosperity of the nation and the height of wage rates depend on a continual increase in the capital invested in its plants, mines and farms, it is one of the foremost tasks of good government to remove all obstacles that hinder the accumulation and investment of new capital."

Ludwig von Mises

Gold stocks offer more leverage than coins or bullion but they also carry more risk. In 1987, when the stock market crashed, gold stocks folded. Another crash may or may not effect gold stocks the same way. It all depends on the price of gold. Since we believe things are bad enough that gold could conceivably go up in every future economic scenario, including a crash, then gold stocks make sense for a portion of one's assets.

For every two dollars you have committed to gold in your physical possession you may wish to speculate with one dollar in gold stocks. First, put at least 10% of your assets into physical coins and bullion before buying gold stocks. Then you will be well situated to put 5% into gold stocks. In this book we are talking about the possibility of our entire economic system coming unglued. Gold stocks can never replace physical gold in such an environment.

Both the U.S. and Canada have come under the influence of strong environmental pressures to halt mining. Further problems with endless permit requirements, regulation, and high taxation, make it difficult to start and run a profitable gold mine in North America. As a result, numerous companies have directed their attention to other parts of the world. Low taxes and recent changes in laws respecting private ownership make South America, Central America, and Mexico, popular with these gold mining companies.

Most of these companies originated in Canada and still have their corporate offices there. Only their field operations exist on foreign soil. Skilled Canadian mining engineers, executives, and geologists, who run these companies know that Mexico and South America are mineral rich and under-explored. New mines built in the past few years testify to the aggressive expansion of the Canadians south of the border.

While political risk exists in South Africa their mines are attractive because of high dividends. In South Africa they aim to mine the gold, pay the proceeds from their gold production out in dividends, and close the company when the mine gives out. The Canadians favor building a long term mining company.

Among the senior companies, you can consider these:

Placer Dome. This company mines 2 1/2 million ounces of gold with some growth expected. They have $300 million and several large working mines. They've had some minor title problems with two excellent prospects in Nevada and Venezuela. If and when these two properties come on stream they should add significantly to production.

Barrick: . This company produces gold at low cost primarily from the Carlin Trend in Nevada. Annual production is over three million ounces. They have new projects in Peru and Chili. They have unrivaled reserves and the lowest cash cost in the industry. Future growth should be strong. This is the premier North American gold miner.

Cambior: This company will mine over 600,000 ounces of gold this year. They have acquired additional production and have a likelihood of developing new mines in Mexico and Peru. Their Omai mine in Guyanna, South America, came on stream without a hitch and produces 350,000 ounces a year. Any company that can develop a problem-free operation right on schedule in a foreign country must know what they are doing.

Battle Mountain: A low-cost Canadian producer with $200 million in cash. They also have silver. This well-managed company produces 900,000 ounces annually. They have two major projects two years away from production and they have major exploration and acquisition programs.

Golden Star. This medium-sized company has a lock on the gold mining areas of Guyana, Surinam, and French Guiana. They own 25 percent of one large producing mine in South America and are aggressively searching for others. They have excellent prospects and could be a major growth company in this decade.

Glamis. This company has capitalized on the new heap leaching technology to become a strong growth story. They have over 100,000 ounces of production currently with more on the way. Their gold reserves were beefed up recently.

Goldcorp. This company owns Wharf Resources and Dickenson Mines. They produce 125,000 ounces a year. The company is led by people of exceptional integrity and skill in every aspect of the gold business. This looks like a safe and sound company.

Here are several junior companies that have good management and solid potential. With higher gold price these could all be substantial winners in the future.

Aurizon. Owns half of two producing mines in Quebec, has acquired a large producing mine recently.

El-Dorado. Aggressive, high growth company active in Mexico and Africa.

Manhattan Minerals. A sound company with a projects in Mexico.

Mansfield Minerals. A first rate exploration company with excellent prospects in Argentina.

These are a few suggestions for you to consider. However, your own research can help you make a decision. Call the companies. Get on their mailing lists. Have them send you financial statements. Talk to the president of the small companies and the investor relations department of the big firms. Look for value and build a portfolio that diversifies and spreads out the risk.

Here are the important newsletters you can subscribe to that give you great coverage on this subject:

Jay Taylor's Gold and Gold Stocks ($89 annually, Box 871, Woodside, NY 11377) This newsletter maintains a sharp focus on a portfolio of Canadian Juniors. Jay's letter manages to dig up a lot of stocks under 25¢ a share. Almost anybody can afford to get size at that price level. Many of his picks have performed well.

Bob Bishop's Gold Stock Newsletter ($159, PO Box 1217, Lafayette, CA 94549-1217) Always good reading that covers a wide portfolio of junior gold and diamond stocks. Bob is a clever guy and his newsletter ranks as the premier publication on gold stocks.

Doug Casey's Crisis Investing ($195, 824 E. Baltimore St., Baltimore, MD 21202) Doug has a big following and he knows his way around the junior gold market and if you get in on his recommendations early it can be profitable. Doug's an original thinker and well worth reading.

Gold Stocks Advisory ($144, PO Box 1437, Burnsville, MN 55337) This letter by Paul Sarnoff covers bigger companies and more conservative gold stock investments with considerable insight. Paul writes an entertaining and worthwhile letter.

Kaiser Bottom-Fishing Report ($99, PO Box 6488, Moraga, CA 94556) John Kaiser is a former Vancouver insider who moved to the U.S. and started a newsletter. He was a successful analyst and knows the players in the mining business. He specializes in the lowest priced stock where the principals have a good reputation. He provides an important insight you can't get anywhere else.

CHAPTER XXV

CULTURE WARS

"It is the greenback which is unstable, and not bullion."

Dr. Franz Pick

"Gold will be around, gold will be money when the dollar and the euro and the yuan and the ringgitt are mere memories."

Richard Russell

"Civilization can only revive when there shall come into being in a number of individuals a new tone of mind independent of the one prevalent among the crowd and in opposition to it. A new public opinion must be created privately and unobtrusively. The existing one is maintained by the press, by propaganda, by organization, and by financial influences which are at its disposal. The unnatural way of spreading ideas must be opposed by the natural one, which goes from man to man and relies solely on the truth of the thoughts and the hearer's receptiveness for new truth."

Albert Schweitzer

Over twenty years ago my late business associate, Bernard Daley, convinced me that there were serious holes in my liberal political views. Bernie politicized me. By the time he died a few years later I held fervent libertarian-conservative views.

Bernie was strongly influenced by the great freedom philosopher, Leonard Read. He followed Read's suggestion that by reading and studying and improving his knowledge of economics and liberty he would radiate greater influence. According to Read, this kind of self-improvement on the part of individual citizens could win the battle between collectivism and capitalism.

Bernie influenced numerous people in a life that was cut short in its prime. Through frequent social get-togethers and discussions he thoroughly politicized them. He would tell me, "It's one mind at a time."

One of the great unrecognized changes in America in the past two decades is the increased politicization of the people. Most of these newly politicized individuals are conservatives or libertarians who have come to possess strong political sentiments. This explains the popularity of conservative talk show hosts. It explains the growing influence of libertarian social and economic thinkers and the renewed clout of conservatives in Washington.

Although conservatives and libertarians are not in harmony on all issues, it's good to remember that there is little dispute on the overriding issues of free markets, limited government, low taxes and liberty. Everyone agrees that the time has come to bury statism and reduce the government. No matter what our religious, personal, social or philosophical views, we must overlook our differences and come together to overturn Leviathan. No less than our civilization and our culture are at stake.

The left has been politicizing its constituents for decades. They have been better at it because early on they captured the schools and the media. They control the institutions. From this vantage point they have initiated a culture war - a direct assault on the old values.

William Bennett tells us in the "DE-VALUING OF AMERICA", "Those whose beliefs govern our institutions will in large measure win the battle for the culture." He quotes Midge Decter, "A culture war, as the liberals understood far better than did their conservative opponents, is a war to the death. For a culture war is not battle over policy, though policy in many cases gives it expres-

146

sion; it is rather a battle about matters of the spirit."

Bennett continues, "So be it. Reclaiming our institutions is less a political opportunity than a civic obligation. It involves hard work. But it is work of immense importance. At the end of the day, somebody's values will prevail."

Often institutions of higher learning lead the assault on our values and culture. Colleges and universities have become the chief domain of the radical left. As Les Csorba writes in Academic License, "The obvious result has been an assault on what we've traditionally called a 'liberal education'. The classical or great books of Western Civilization, which teach virtue, order and civility, and which lie as the political foundation of our constitutional republic have been attacked by academic disciples fostering new truly quasi-academic disciplines such as 'Peace Studies'..... and so on." Shakespeare and Cervantes are replaced with obscure, minority female poets. Marxism, a miserable economic and social failure is alive and well within American universities.

If you wonder why a simple prayer in school causes such a fuss; why quotas and affirmative action were stuffed down your throat; why the Smithsonian Institution takes the side of the Japanese in World War II; why Columbus suddenly became a stinker; or why sweeping legislation such as the American Disabilities Act is rammed through without any thought about the astronomical financial consequences, you can be sure it all started with the liberal intellectuals infesting the universities who want to hold sway over our culture.

The left has made its mark. This is the age of excess; a nation of overweight citizens on a runaway consumption binge; a failing educational system; the dumbing down of youth; bizarre people in public places with rings in their tongues; a staggering boom in fun, self indulgence and entertainment; endless examples of bad taste and vulgarity and shameless citizens sharing degrading personal revelations on TV.

Along with these extremes comes a plague of crime. In today's cities murders barely make the news. An overworked court system is strained to breaking because of its own leniency. Nasty examples of theft such as shoplifting and stealing cars get no more punishment than a traffic ticket. Drug violations are the common cold of a sick court system and ten or fifteen drunk driving charges may get you a year in jail with 9 months suspended.

Writing about the decay of the American character (and culture), Charles J. Sykes explains, "Something extraordinary is happening in American society. Crisscrossed by invisible trip wires of emotional, racial, sexual and psychological grievance, American life is increasingly characterized by the plaintive insistence, I am a victim......the mantra of the victims is the same: I am not responsible, it's not my fault."

The left has promoted massive subsidies and runaway social programs that encourage this mindset. People believe they deserve something for nothing. They are victims. They rationalize a free ride. They are told the playing field isn't level, that merit is a scam, that values are subjective, that doing nothing is no better or worse than building and creating.

An employer sees it all: the fraudulent unemployment claims, the refusal to work, the unwillingness to do extra; the bogus lawsuits that encourage neurosis. Spurred by large legal awards, more and more people look for ways to sue and depict themselves as victims.

Left-wing social policies sicken our behavior and corrupt our culture. People bend principles and sacrifice integrity to get as much as they can from the government. Giveaway programs encourage every imaginable sort of cheating and dishonesty. Wheeling and dealing in food stamps is a way of life. Lying and fraud are commonplace. Whenever you're dependent on the money, the end justifies the means.

Many people enrolled in one government program or another work part time for cash at either a legitimate job or illegal activity. By taking payments in cash they don't show any income and can maintain their benefits. The numbers of people working the system this way are legion.

Money dispersed without any requirement to earn it seems to set off a defensive reaction wherein the recipients claim a right to the money almost like a state pensioner or a person who has purchased an annuity. It creates an attitude problem. A friend tells of sitting in a doctor's office when an unemployed man became insulted because he was asked if he worked. He angrily emphasized that he would never work.

A certain segment of the population will always succumb to the lure of a free ride. When a bad back became a way to secure long-term workmen's compensation benefits, the number of bad backs per capita went through the roof. Payments to those who can't find work will snare many who can find work. Subsidies carry incentives that encourage the rewarded behavior. Payments for unemployment spread unemployment. Payments to alleviate poverty spread poverty.

Free health care provides another example. Hospital emergency rooms are clogged with people with minor or imagined afflictions. Free insurance bids up the costs of health care by increasing demand. It discourages good health and promotes ill health. In 1936, Ludwig von Mises wrote in his book, SOCIALISM, "If the will to be well and efficient is weakened, illness and inability to work is caused..... In short, (social health insurance) is an institution which tends to encourage disease, not to say accidents and to intensify considerably the physical and psychic results of accidents and illnesses. As a social institution it makes a people sick bodily and mentally or at least helps to multiply, lengthen and intensify disease." Free money promoted by the left is a curse on our culture.

My old associate, Bernie, was ahead of his time. Years ago he knew what was coming. He worked to improve his knowledge and understanding, influenced everyone he could reach, made friends and allies, fiercely opposed the inroads of the state and joined to the fullest extent the struggle against the left. He was pessimistic about the nation's future and once confided in me, "Jimmy, we are going to hit the gutter." But he knew there was hope and in the dawn of the culture wars, he fought to his last breath.

CHAPTER XXVI

A FULL BLOWN
ECONOMIC COLLAPSE

"In brief, the jig is about up and painless extrication from our predicament just isn't going to be possible."

Alfred A. Malabre, Jr.

"How rare is gold? If you could gather together all the gold mined in recorded history, melt it down, and pour it into one giant cube, it would measure only about eighteen yards across! That's all the gold owned by every government on earth, plus all the gold in private hands, all the gold in rings, necklaces, chains, and gold art. That's all the gold used in tooth fillings, in electronics, in coins and bars. It's everything that exists above ground now, or since man learned to extract the metal from the earth. All of it can fit into one block the size of a single house. It would weigh about 91,000 tons - less than the amount of steel made around the world in an hour. That's rare."

Daniel M. Kehrer

"Bullion doesn't pay interest or dividends, nor does it grow or expand by itself. That's the price you pay for tranquillity."

Pierre Lassonde

People cannot foresee the things they don't want to happen. In other words, your interest and need for some other outcome make it unlikely you will be ready for an economic shock. It's human nature. No matter how inevitable it may be, most people won't see a crash coming. Because the full fury of a market and currency collapse will strike you so unexpectedly you stand to be devastated by it. Every paper asset you own, everything you count on, and everything that has been promised you for your retirement can be swept away in a torrent of fear and panic. In the long economic history of the world, no nation's economy or paper money has escaped the pitiless repudiations, failures, depressions, shocks, devaluations, hyper-inflations, and bankruptcies, that have remorselessly wiped out the gullible citizenry.

For 30 years, various soothsayers have issued warnings of a frightful economic crash. So far they have proven to be wrong. Many people use this as a reason to scoff at such warnings. Because no severe economic crisis has afflicted us in recent memory does not mean that such an event can't occur. In fact, the reasons these warnings were issued remain very much intact, and, in all cases, are more serious than before. The day of reckoning may have been postponed but it only has served to compound the problem.

The U.S. emphasizes consuming over saving. We are the grasshoppers fiddling away the summer while elsewhere the ants save and invest. This policy of eating the seed corn was promoted by (wouldn't you know it) liberal economists. Other more noteworthy economists refer to such policies as the prescription for national disaster.

The gargantuan U.S. current account deficit of $170 billion last year, on top of fourteen years of huge deficits can't go on. By glutting the world with dollars, we export our consumer inflation and run down the dollar. The rest of the world has let us get by with this. But it is a policy that cannot last. Most likely, the dollar faces a disastrous devaluation.

It gets worse. The total of public and private debt now stands at $16 trillion. These astronomical debt levels mean that we have overextended ourselves beyond our underlying collateral or beyond our ability to repay. The interest payments on this debt eat up a dangerous share of annual income. These unprecedented debt levels dwarf anything in history.

The huge debt buildup accounts for the strong financial markets of the 1990's. Buying securities on borrowed money returned handsome profits. This leveraging carries risks of historic proportions. Wall Street doesn't seem to care. How else could the highest stock valuations in history coexist with such low savings and investment levels?

America lives beyond its means. Long term trends in profits, incomes, savings, and investments, are unhealthy. Runaway consumption, debt, and speculation, on top of soaring trade deficits, can't be sustained. They threaten a financial disaster of a magnitude that exceeds anything in history.

Money and credit trends give even more cause for alarm. Monetary easing and declining long-term interest rates fuel a boom in mortgage refinancing and consumer borrowing. This, along with reduced savings and stock gains propel spending and economic growth. A huge credit bubble in lockstep with a huge speculative stock market bubble lays at the core of U.S. economic strength. Should the stock market bubble burst, the economy will be next. Attempts to save the economy and the stock market through lower interest rates promise further deterioration of the dollar.

Most of U.S. corporate profits are derived from short-term gains from lower interest costs, reduced taxes, slow depreciation growth, huge stock buybacks and reduced payroll costs from the use of stock options. Outside of high-tech, productive capital investment has been replaced by financial speculation. Profit erosion seems inevitable. Any divergence from the rosiest of scenarios will put the vulnerable consumer in severe financial straits and end the borrowing binge. Bankruptcies are already at record high levels.

Massive exposure to derivative risk by U.S. banks in another alarming trend. Major banks appear to be speculating heavily in currency and derivative markets. Balance sheets are burdened with financial leverage and astonishing levels of derivative risk that require liquid international markets to unwind positions. Further deterioration in Asia or elsewhere could be disastrous.

Another problem of late is that the huge growth in debt did not materialize through bank lending but through massive lending by non-bank financial institutions (brokerage firms - corporations). This multiplies credit and debt without adding to the money stock. Money (liquidity) is the necessary ingredient for repayments. In other words, the money supply has been grossly overleveraged through speculative excess in financial markets and a massive debt buildup by non-bank lenders. These credit distortions contribute to the possibility of a liquidity crisis, debt meltdown, and crashing securities markets.

Here's a likely scenario in this worst of all worlds: A surging economic recovery gives way to profit declines and a slumping economy. This triggers a crashing stock market and a plunging dollar. A weakening currency drives up interest rates and collapses the bond market. All asset values shrivel, and the soaring cost of imports sends consumer inflation into orbit. A dreaded inflationary depression and market collapse destroys the accumulated wealth of the people.

Sounds far fetched? Not at all. Gloomy financial trends can't be brushed aside. Our economic sins are real. They defy ready solutions. Consequently, you can lose enormously on your paper assets. Your retirement and savings plans can be devastated. The government can be overwhelmed trying to cover guarantees and losses, to say nothing of trying to solve its own debt and currency problems. What passes for economic normalcy in America today is pure folly. Once it begins to unravel in earnest and the monetary authorities lose control, then comes panic.

Only a few can see the dry rot undermining our financial affairs. Even the newsletters and authors who made their names warning of such crises have grown silent. The students of the great Austrian economists now give bullish financial advice and their subscribers go naked into the cataclysm. *People cannot foresee the things they don't want to happen.*

Here's another revelation: *Only those who can benefit from a future event have any chance of forecasting it.* Their minds are open to it and they often contemplate it. It's our view that some of the ugliest chapters in the history of economics are imminent in America. The thought of such an economic crisis may have crossed your mind. You may have a vague sense of unease. However, it is terribly difficult to comprehend this possibility when you need the future to be positive in order to accomplish your goals. *An economic earthquake will hurt those people the worst who have the most to lose.* More than ever you need to consider how to protect yourself.

Gold is the only asset that protects you from virtually every economic danger. You need gold. It can save you. At a minimum put 10% of your net worth into gold. In light of the current problems I urge you to think about putting 20% into gold. Present economic dangers suggest the bottom could fall out of other assets and markets at any time. You have little to lose. In five, 10 or 20 years the historical evidence argues that you will be able to sell your gold and get back at least what you put into it in terms of purchasing power.

CHAPTER XXVII

WHAT YOU SHOULD DO NOW

"At a minimum, gold will rise to $3,000. A more likely scenario, however, is that the world's financial system will break down completely. (The basis of that system is the U.S. dollar.) In that case, gold will rise as high as $10,000 to $40,000 - a point at which all credit - paper will be backed by gold."

Steve Puetz

"Start buying gold now, regardless of the price. By acting now, you will not have to react when it's too late. Too late will be when the majority of the public finally figures out what is happening to paper money and frantically tries to get aboard. Remember, if you're one of the ones holding paper in the end, you will have given away your products and services for nothing."

Robert Ringer

"Gold is not less but more rational than paper money. Money holds value so long as it is in limited supply; gold will always be in limited supply, and would require real resources to produce even from the sea; paper and printing ink are not in limited supply. The gold system is much closer to a modern automatic scientific control system than the crude and relatively unstable system of paper."

William Rees-Mogg

Review the following paragraphs to completely understand everything that gold does for you.

- *If you purchased gold 20 years ago it will still buy the same amount of goods today that it did back then.*

- *Gold preserves purchasing power. You can't say that about stocks or bonds with any degree of certainty.*

- *Gold prices don't fluctuate much. Actually, gold should be considered a conservative holding. With the exception of two years (1974 and 1980), gold has had little or no price volatility in hundreds of years.*

- *When the Asian currencies recently lost half their value Asians who owned gold lost nothing. Gold offsets the loss of currency values. Like Asia, the U.S. borrows, inflates and spends to excess.*

- *The absolute liquidity of gold means it can be turned into cash virtually anywhere in the world.*

- *Lawsuits and judgments can strip you of your assets. Stock, bonds and real estate are highly visible. Gold stays hidden.*

- *Gold doesn't need a strong financial statement. Annuities and bonds depend on the financial strength of the issuer. The value of gold requires no outside solvency.*

- *Gold is recognized and cherished everywhere in the world. No other asset carries such universal recognition and respect.*

- *Unlike real estate or art objects, a high concentration of gold values can be stored in a small place. Gold is easily hidden and highly portable.*

- *Gold makes a private high value gift to be given to heirs and passed on to loved ones.*

- *In a deflation or asset collapse, gold tends to lose less value than other assets. In the depression, gold was revalued from $18 to $36 an ounce.*

- *In cases of national emergencies, wars, disasters, civil unrest, and financial crisis, gold saves lives, provides comforts, and secures passage.*

- *Gold has the world's longest track record. Four thousand years of evidence proves that nothing else compares. Other assets invariably deteriorate, fail, change, or pass away.*

- *Up until this century, gold was the world's money. It was the perfect medium of exchange, unit of account, and store of value. No other asset comes close to meeting the definition of money.*

- *Gold protects you like nothing else. If every financial asset that you own goes down the drain you can take your gold out and recapture what you put into it. Gold can save your lifestyle.*

- *A store of gold acts as a savings plan. Monthly purchases of gold build asset value and can be used as a private retirement program.*

Once you have made a decision you want to know more about the types of gold available to you and the current prices, I suggest you immediately call Investment Rarities Inc. at 1-800-328-1860. Ask for a broker. That person will answer any questions you might have and make sure you receive their regular newsletter on gold and economics.

Next you should think about how much you want to put into gold. I suggest 10% to 20% of your net worth. If things get bad in the economy you may ultimately wish to go higher.

You also need to consider where to keep your gold. A bank safe deposit box will do. (In the 1930's when the banks closed, the safe deposit boxes were still available for entry.) You should also contemplate the purchase of a home safe. This should be built-in or hidden in a basement or closet. This makes an excellent place to store your gold.

Once you own $500,000 in gold you may wish to store some overseas. I can think of no finer nest egg than to have $1,000,000 in gold bars or coins stored in a Swiss vault or in a Swiss bank deposit box. It's quite a simple process to make such an arrangement. Naturally, only a few people can afford such measures. But for those who can, the storage of gold in Switzerland has a lot going for it. This island of security should offset the worst kind of unexpected crisis.

Here are three portfolios we recommend:

Portfolio #1 - $10,000

$5,000 Philharmonics (1 ounce gold coins)

$5,000 U.S. Double Eagles ($20 gold pieces) Saint-Gaudens variety.

Portfolio #2 - $50,000

$10,000 Philharmonics or U.S. Eagles

$20,000 Saint-Gaudens Double Eagles AU to MS-62 grade

$10,000 $20 Liberty Head Double Eagles XF to MS-62 grade

$5,000 Modern U.S. gold Commemoratives
($5 Statue of Liberty, $5 Constitution, etc.)

$ 5,000 $10 U.S. gold Liberty Eagles or Indians in circulated condition

Portfolio #3 - $100,000

$20,000 Philharmonics, U.S. Eagles or Krugerrands.

$40,000 Saint-Gaudens Double Eagles MS-61 grade

$20,000 $20 Liberty Head Double Eagles Extremely Fine Grade

$10,000 $5 Liberty Head Half Eagles Circulated Grades

$10,000 Modern U.S. gold Commemoratives or small foreign pieces

I fear that any great demand for gold will make the antique U.S. gold pieces (Double Eagles, Eagles and Half-Eagles) difficult to get. When markets are dull these coins are plentiful, but any dramatic increase in demand would probably dry up the supply. If you read Chapter XX, "The Best Gold Collector Coins," you will see many of the reasons they are so popular. If these coins become too scarce or too expensive you will need to buy the more available pieces or newly minted coins.

Don't hesitate to act on these suggestions. Any delay could prove to be a mistake in judgment. With what I think we face you are incalculably better off to be early than late. If you forego some interest or a gain on something else, that's the price of your peace of mind.

I leave you with these thoughts:

No country ever edged further out on a financial limb than the U.S. The gargantuan debt, the leveraging, the trade, and budget deficits, don't represent some new sort of progress or advanced economic strategy. They are as old as man, and whenever they have been practiced so wantonly, an enormous price has been paid. We trifle with laws that we don't fully understand. The sorry outcome is as clear to me as it is inevitable.

Henry Hazlitt summed it up nicely. "There are men regarded today as brilliant economists, who deprecate saving and recommend squandering on a national scale as the way of economic salvation; and when anyone points to what the consequences of these policies will be in the long run, they reply flippantly, as might the prodigal son of a warning father: 'In the long run we are all dead.' And such shallow wisecracks pass as devastating epigrams and ripest wisdom.

"But the tragedy is that, on the contrary, we are already suffering the long-run consequences of the policies of the remote or recent past. Today is already the tomorrow which the bad economist yesterday urged us to ignore. The long-run consequences of some economic policies may become evident in a few months. Others may not become evident for several years. Still others may not become evident for decades. But in every case those long-run consequences are contained in the policy as surely as the hen was in the egg, the flower in the seed."

What we don't know and can't know involves the degree of the coming crunch. A severe decline differs from a total collapse. Suffice to say that something bad must come from all of this economic sinfulness. But also remember that our superstructure of debt along with all the other economic distortions holds the potential to create a black hole of asset destruction. Even those who own a lot of gold or who profit through selling gold will shrink from this dire outcome.

Also, it's worth remembering that most people in this country don't have enough assets to protect themselves from anything truly bad. They can afford but a pittance in precious metals. Furthermore, these people will never believe that they should own gold, no matter what. Therefore, if jobs, government safety nets and retirement assets vanish, most people are finished. In the 1930's the government had the financial clout to mitigate the damage. This time it could be different. Such an outcome has the potential to set off an orgy of redistribution.

Finally, if you have read this far you may be in the unique position to be able to buy enough gold to protect yourself and secure your future in an angry and unhappy country. Own your gold quietly, don't confide in friends or relatives who may accidentally disclose this information, and rely on gold before anything else as your insurance against the events predicted in this book. Nothing else will do. Foreign bonds and currencies or other tangible assets are not a proxy for gold. Remember that paper is man's money but gold is nature's money.

As some of our predictions begin to unfold, the yellow metal will experience a newfound popularity. The experts in the media, government, and Wall Street, will express amazement at the powerful revival of interest in gold. At some point, the monetary authorities may even look to gold to bail them out of the mess that they made with paper money. Quite possibly gold will perform the money function once again. One thing is for sure: gold will make a great comeback.

Coins Pictured

Front Cover—20 St. Gaudens

Back Cover—Vienna Philharmonic

The opinions in this book represent my views on gold, economics and the future. Since I am a human being, my insights must be limited and prone to error. I have made many mistakes in the past and have sometimes been wrong on similar issues to those covered in this book. If acted upon, my advice represents a significant departure from current financial norms. Many experts consider a commitment to gold to be risky and unprofitable. I have a conflict of interest in conveying advice about gold since I am also the principal gold dealer in America. As such I would have obvious prejudices. I cannot guarantee the accuracy of all the information in this book, and the facts it provides can be incomplete or condensed. Although I believe gold to be the best thing for a person to own in this country today and that gold can save people from a horrible financial fate, I stress that I can be wrong about this. It's possible that none of the events I predict will come to pass, that the future will be rosy and that gold will be less relevant. The sole purpose of this book is to educate the reader about gold with the intent of convincing the reader to buy gold.

JAMES R. COOK is President of Investment Rarities Incorporated. He is the author of *Windows for Grandparents* and *The Start-up Entrepreneur,* a best-selling business book. He has appeared on FNN, CNN, the Regis Philbin Show, the Larry King Show, and the Today Show. He lives in Minneapolis, Minnesota.

INDEX

Skousen, Mark, 115
Smith, Jerome F., 13
Smithsonian Institution, 147
Sobran, Joseph, 88
South Africa, 15, 21, 133, 140
South America, 14, 134, 136, 140, 141
Soviet Union, 130
Spain, 14
Spanish, 10
Stalin, 91, 110
Surinam, 141
Sutton, Antony C., 13
Swiss Franc, 107
Switzerland, 103
Sykes, Charles J., 148

- T -
Taiwan, 135
The Heritage Foundation, 79
The Pas, 53
The Territorial Imperative, 41
Tort Reform, 59
Troy, 11
Turk, James, 30
Turkey, 12

- U -
U.S., 6, 9, 19-21, 23, 29, 44, 68, 69,
   74, 75, 78, 82, 89, 94-97, 106, 110,
   111, 113, 116, 121-123, 130, 131,
   133, 134, 140, 143, 152, 153
U.S. Central Bank, 24
U.S. Double Eagles, 161
U.S. Eagles, 110
U.S. Gold Eagle, 105
U.S. Government, 77
U.S. Indians, 161
U.S. Mint, 18
Utt, Ronald, 79

- V -
VA & FHA Mortgages, 80

Velasquez, 14
Venezuela, 141
Venice, 13
Vienna Philharmonic, 106
von Hayak, F.A., 39
von Mises Ludwig, 29, 33-39, 57, 63,
   67, 83, 87, 105, 109, 139, 149

- W -
Wall Street, 117
Webster, Daniel, 63
Weil, Gordon L., 19
Western Europe, 13
World War II, 19
Wounded Knee, 52

- Y -
Yukon, 15